W9-CHS-329

UP

UP

DEVOTIONS FOR FAITH THAT CONNECTS

tim baker and jenn doucette

Revell

Grand Rapids, Michigan

© 2007 by Tim Baker and Jenn Doucette

Published by Fleming H. Revell
a division of Baker Publishing Group
P.O. Box 6287, Grand Rapids, MI 49516-6287
www.revellbooks.com

Printed in the United States of America

All rights reserved. No part of this publication may be reproduced, stored in a retrieval system, or transmitted in any form or by any means—for example, electronic, photocopy, recording—without the prior written permission of the publisher. The only exception is brief quotations in printed reviews.

Library of Congress Cataloging-in-Publication Data
Baker, Tim, 1965–
    Up : devotions for faith that connects / Tim Baker and Jenn Doucette.
        p.   cm.
    ISBN 10: 0-8007-5883-8 (pbk.)
    ISBN 978-0-8007-5883-7 (pbk.)
    1. Teenagers—Religious life. 2. Teenagers—Prayers and devotions. 3. Christian life. 4. Spiritual life. I. Doucette, Jenn, 1969– II. Title.
    BV4531.3.B35 2007
    242'.63—dc22   2007003083

Unless otherwise indicated, Scripture is taken from the HOLY BIBLE, NEW INTERNATIONAL VERSION®. NIV®. Copyright © 1973, 1978, 1984 by International Bible Society. Used by permission of Zondervan. All rights reserved.

Scripture is also taken from *The Message* by Eugene H. Peterson, copyright © 1993, 1994, 1995, 2000, 2001, 2002. Used by permission of NavPress Publishing Group. All rights reserved.

From Jenn—
For J.J., Katie & Emma

From Tim—
For Nicole, Jessica & Jacob

Contents

Acknowledgments

Jenn—

I would like to thank my coauthor, Tim Baker, for giving me the privilege of working on this book with him. Many thanks go to my agent, Chip MacGregor, for being the amazing go-between-guy that he is.

I am grateful to my loving and supportive husband, Ben; if he hadn't moved himself and the kids out of the house for a long weekend, I never would have met my deadline. Thanks for "takin' it for the team," babe—I'll always love you!

I am also thankful to my three kiddos, J.J., Katie, and Emma, who think it's cool that their mom writes books. You are my greatest treasures; may you live your lives connecting with the One who loves you even more than I do: Jesus.

Tim—

Okay, Jenn took a lot of the really good acknowledgments. This next paragraph is going to sound like a repeat.

Thanks to Jenn Doucette for coming alongside me with this project. You're a great writer, Jenn.

Thanks to Chip MacGregor for connecting the dots for me. (See, I told you she took the good ones!).

My wife and kids sacrifice time and countless potential adventures to let me write and create. You're an incredible family. I love you!

The entire editorial staff at Baker Publishing Group for their hard work. Jennifer Leep—thanks for your willingness to take these books on and your unending patience.

Introduction

It's just you, five bucks, and your favorite fast-food place.

It's been forever since you've been back to your favorite fast-food place. Too much to do at school, church, and home have kept you from getting back to the burgers you love. Standing there at the counter, you notice that the menu has changed. New burgers are accompanied by salad options, different kinds of fries, and a strange array of chicken value meals. There are cheese- and chili-covered this-and-thats. Each new item is advertised with a picture. The new hot dog photograph makes it look like a "thirty-ton missile meal." The bacon-covered hamburger picture promises what looks like forty-five pounds of beef with a skyscraper-sized pile of pickles, tomatoes, lettuce, etc.

The sign on the wall to your left explains it all: "Under New Management." And even though the entire place is totally new, you decide to go for it. The pictures tell the whole story about your meal, and the story sounds good.

You walk to the counter and lay your money out like it's a prom queen on display. This is your five dollars. This is the result of your hard work. You feel good about letting the cash go, especially because of the promises the pictures make. You order the #2 Extra Big Value-Sized Meal with an almost half-gallon cup filled with your favorite soft drink. And no sooner have you ordered it than the tray arrives on the counter in front of you. As you look down to check out your meal, you hear the cashier say, "Thanks for coming, and you come back to see us again."

Walking away, you're immediately aware of the irony. So much so, that you look back toward the counter and focus on the poster to the right of the lighted menu panels. There, on the front wall, is the picture of the meal you have lying on your tray. The poster portrays this huge burger; the burger on your tray is about the size of half your fist. The poster fries look crispy and hot and just salted enough; the fries on your tray are obviously undercooked and oversalted.

Finding the only clean seat in the place, you sit and begin to unpack your #2 Extra Big Value-Sized Meal. The meal is less than you expected. Way less. It's less than the advertisement.

The burger doesn't look anything like the picture. Unsure . . . maybe you're remembering wrong. You look up at the huge poster advertising your meal. There it is. Fries and drink with this huge mountain of a hamburger. The one in the picture is perfect. Everything is just right. Ketchup perfectly dripping off the edge. You look down. Your burger looks more like an old, overused doorstop.

The meat patty is overcooked, there's too much ketchup, no pickles—and all of that piled on a bun that should have been retired three days ago.

As your wreck of a lunch lays there—a dead hamburger patty in an open bun casket—you're frustrated. The picture was a lie. The promise made by the advertisement doesn't match the actual product. This is "realness" in reverse. The picture preaches one thing, the real-life sample an entirely different story. The message and the product don't match.

I wonder, have you ever lived this way? It's an easy trap to fall into. We sometimes proclaim a message we can't live up to. We preach one way with our mouths and preach another message with our lives. We make a promise or claim a promise or identify ourselves with people who make promises about what their lifestyle is like, and then our actual lives don't match up. Our advertising, words, and promises are attractive, but our lives are a total lie. False advertising. Realness in reverse.

What's up with that? We've reverted to a sanctified version of our former selves and have readopted our sinful mind-set. We proclaim an allegiance to Christ, but our lives are sloppy. We're overcooked versions of the truth. Our lives don't match the picture Christ painted for people who follow him. The truth we say we believe doesn't connect with the lives we lead.

Up: Devotions for Faith That Connects is designed to help you match your life actions to your identity in Christ. Work out your walk, strengthen your spirit, and beef up your soul. This book is about making that vertical connection—putting your body, attitude, heart, and power in God's hands. In his hands, you can have a faith and life that connect. In his hands, you can live it real.

HOW Do You Use This Book?

We've put this book together so you'll be able to use it in one of two ways. You can work through all twelve chapters in twelve weeks, or you can tackle it on your own, at your own pace. If you choose the weekly alternative, you'll notice the following format:

Day 1: This day is more challenging and usually asks you to write down your own ideas about a topic after reflecting on Scripture.

Days 2–5: These days generally hang out on the topic for the week and help you understand more about the topic.

Day 6: This day gives you a situation you might encounter and asks you to try to apply what you've learned throughout the week to the topic.

Day 7: The last day of the week you get to have a little fun. These are usually simple activities that help illustrate the theme for the week.

Really, it doesn't matter how you use this book. Before you sit down and begin, though, here's a little advice about having devotions.

1. Find a good time. You've got to read God's Word when you're most awake and alert. Some people are alive at 6:30 a.m., and they're firing on all their cylinders. Truth is, not everyone is like that. If you aren't alert in the morning, don't have devos then. Think about when you're most alert, and give God your time when he'll get you at your best.

2. Find a good place. You're not a copy. Everyone doesn't learn the same way, or in the same environment. Do your friends talk about how they read their Bibles before they go to bed? Have you ever wondered why you don't remember anything you read before you go to bed, but your friends do? Maybe your bed isn't the best place for you to read. Give some thought to the best place for you to read God's Word. Find a place where you'll be able to focus.

3. Pray. Lots of times we talk about how prayer after devotions is important. Truth is, prayer at the beginning is important too. Before you open God's Word, remember to ask him to guide your mind to what he wants you to learn.

4. Mark where you've been. Always keep a pencil handy. Keep one in your Bible. As you read through God's Word, mark things you think are interesting. If you do that, you'll know where you've been in God's Word, and over time you'll create some valuable notes in your Bible.

The most important thing about devotions is that you have them. It can be tough to keep a schedule of reading God's Word. It takes real discipline! Hopefully this book will help you stay consistent in your devotional life and will challenge you to live God's Word without fear.

God bless you in your journey through this book and in your walk with Christ.

WHY SHOULD I BE HONEST WITH GOD?

DAY 1

The LORD will keep you from all harm—he will watch over your life; the LORD will watch over your coming and going both now and forevermore.

Psalm 121:7–8

The LORD is gracious and compassionate; slow to anger and rich in love.

Psalm 145:8

Surely you desire truth in the inner parts; you teach me wisdom in the inmost place.

Psalm 51:6

Want to know something about God?

He sees everything.

I know, not rocket science. Probably something you already knew. I guess that's not new information.

But when you think about it, God is the last person we expect to be watching us. We rarely think about how God is watching us when we're messing up in a huge way. Or even in a small way. We hope God's looking when we're volunteering at a soup kitchen, having our devotions, or telling others about him. But we ignore the fact that he's still watching when we aren't doing something great.

This week we're getting honest with God. By the end of the week, you'll hopefully be a few steps closer to being 100 percent honest with God about every area of your life. To get you started in your quest for honesty, let's start with just a little bit of honesty right at the very beginning of the week. Take a few moments and write down four things you'd like to confess to God that you haven't already.

- _____
- _____
- _____
- _____

Was that easy?

Chances are, if you're the type of person to look through a devotional book, you're more than ready to do some serious soul searching—even if it reveals some less-than-stellar results in the honesty department. This week let's commit to being totally honest with the only person who knows you better than anyone does, even your parents. They may claim to have eyes in the back of their head, but remember—God sees *everything*.

↑ Looking Up

What are some of the good things in your life God sees?

What are some of the bad things in your life God sees?

How does your view of your earthly father impact your vision of your heavenly Father?

DAY 2

Jesus answered, "I am the way and the truth and the life. No one comes to the Father except through me."

John 14:6

Two things I ask of you, O Lord; do not refuse me before I die: Keep falsehood and lies far from me; give me neither poverty nor riches, but give me only my daily bread. Otherwise, I may have too much and disown you and say, "Who is the Lord?"

Proverbs 30:7–9

If we claim to have fellowship with him yet walk in the darkness, we lie and do not live by the truth.

1 John 1:6

"What is truth?"

This, a loaded question asked of Jesus by Pilate only hours before he ordered him crucified. Earlier in the book of John, Jesus said to his disciples, "I am the way and the truth and the life." Outside of Jesus, can truth be defined? How about honesty? Both imply a level of correctness, accuracy, and precision.

However, honesty says more about the *inner* workings of a person (and I'm *not* talking about second-period hunger pangs). It conjures up words like *integrity*, *honor*, and *sincerity*. Kind of like the feeling you get when you hear the national anthem in a packed stadium sporting a winning home team. In a philosophical equation of sorts, it's like this:

goodness + decency = honesty

So what does that leave those of us who are . . . dishonest? Corrupt? Evil? In a spiritual sense, yes. "For all have sinned and fall short of the glory of God" (Romans 3:23), right? But for those of us who have accepted Jesus's sacrifice in payment for all our wrongs, God no longer views us as sinful.

Whew. Major bullet dodge. Oh, we still sin. Every day, in fact. But if we confess those sins, we are forgiven. Totally forgiven. Talk about unconditional love. So what's holding you back? If God already sees and knows everything, and he'll forgive each and every petty (not to mention humongous) sin, what's keeping you from being completely honest with him?

Reflect on the verses above again. Write down two things that prevent you from being completely honest with God.

- _____
- _____

OK, now that you're in a groove, write down two more.

- _____
- _____

The fact is, there are a lot of things that keep us from being completely honest with God. Once you can identify those and bring them before him in prayer, then you'll be on your way toward an honest relationship with your Creator.

Never forget that God can handle any truth you throw at him. In fact, he already knows it. Question: So what is truth? Answer: God is truth.

↑ Looking Up

In the past, what kinds of sins did you think were unforgivable?

How do you think it makes God feel (yes, he is a person—he does feel!) when you try to hide your sins from him?

How can the sin of dishonesty with God stunt your spiritual growth?

DAY 3

To the Jews who had believed him, Jesus said, "If you hold to my teaching, you are really my disciples. Then you will know the truth, and the truth will set you free."

John 8:31–32

So if the Son sets you free, you will be free indeed.

John 8:36

But now that you have been set free from sin and have become slaves to God, the benefit you reap leads to holiness, and the result is eternal life. For the wages of sin is death, but the gift of God is eternal life in Christ Jesus our Lord.

Romans 6:22–23

I learned an interesting fact about circus elephants. While they are young, they undergo training that leads to a condition known as *learned helplessness*. Here's how it works: when an elephant is little (a mere 300 pounds) he is attached to heavy chains that are staked into the ground. The baby elephant inevitably chafes at the loss of freedom when he realizes he cannot break free from his confinement.

Once the elephant learns his limitations in regard to the chain, he can be restrained with only the use of a thin rope. The trainer knows that the use of chains and stakes are no longer needed. Even after the elephant is full grown (an impressive 8,000–12,000 pounds) and has more than enough strength to pull the stake out of the ground, he stops trying because he still believes that he is helpless to overcome his captivity.

Satan would like nothing better than for you to see yourself as helpless to overcome your past sins. He works tirelessly to wrap your mistakes around your leg and stake them to the ground with shame and guilt. For many people, once they've been trained not to resist his taunts, they become forever imprisoned by their burden of sin.

That's not to downplay the impact of sin in the slightest. Let's be very clear about the fact that sin is huge and separates us from God. And in our own power, we are truly unable to break free from its stronghold. However, once we've moved from the darkness to the light, our sins are as puny as dental floss around the leg of a 12,000-pound elephant.

What breaks the cycle of learned helplessness and being held captive to sin? Need you ask? It is being honest with the Lord about these sins. It is confessing them to him in a genuine posture of repentance.

Think about some of the guilt trips you've traveled on your life journey. Write down how your "captivity" has hindered a healthy and vibrant relationship with God.

_____

_____

_____

God doesn't want to make your chains stronger. He wants to set you free. Stop trying to break free on your own. And don't be like a circus elephant—there's a lot more of life to live outside the Big Top.

In what ways does our unconfessed sin please Satan?

Why does confessing our sin please God?

What steps have you taken toward finding true freedom in Christ?

DAY 4

The LORD is my rock, my fortress and my deliverer; my God is my rock in whom I take refuge. He is my shield and the horn of my salvation, my stronghold. I call to the LORD, who is worthy of praise, and I am saved from my enemies.

Psalm 18:2–3

Trust in the LORD forever, for the LORD, the LORD, is the Rock eternal.

Isaiah 26:4

"Can anyone hide in secret places so that I cannot see him?" declares the LORD. "Do not I fill heaven and earth?" declares the LORD.

Jeremiah 23:24

OK, take a deep breath. This being completely honest with God ain't for the faint of heart. Actor George Burns once said, "The most important thing in acting is honesty. If you can fake that, you've got it made."*

While this may be true in television la-la land, we've learned that we can't fake it in the real world with God. That's because of the three Oms. Never heard of them? Here they are:

1. God is *Omniscient*—(remember from Day 1?) He is all-knowing.
2. God is *Omnipresent*—He is present in all places at the same time.
3. God is *Omnipotent*—He is all-powerful.

---

* George Burns, Bartleby.com, http://www.bartleby.com/63/17/6117.html, October 7, 2004.

That's a lot of Oms, isn't it? The significance of the Oms is that NOTHING YOU DO SURPRISES GOD. While some of your activities may turn your mom a little green, God cannot be shocked—he is the Unshockable Rock.

Kinda takes the pressure off a little, doesn't it? You don't have to work up the courage to tell God about your failings. The truth is, there is nothing you can do to drive God away. Your sin won't drive him away because his Son's death covered the penalty for it. This may seem like a basic concept, one you've heard many times before; but there are millions of people throughout history who have run from God because they couldn't get over their own sin.

Apparently they didn't know about the Oms.

You do. Now what are you going to do about it?

The task of being real before God may take some practice. We've become all too good at faking honesty with those around us. Our society doesn't like to hear about problems and mistakes. They call things like that *issues*.

Relax. God sees these sins for what they are—and he's the only one who is able to deal with them. Let's think of some more Oms, shall we?

God is omni-loving. Omni-patient. Omni-forgiving.

Now it's your turn. Think of some characteristics of God and fill in the blanks below. The prefix "omni" means "a combining form meaning all."

Omni _trustworthy_
Omni _Protector_
Omni _teacher_

↑ Looking Up

As Christians, why is it important to be honest with God and with one another?

How does hypocrisy (fakin' our faith) rob us of a relationship with God?

Can you think of some honest, real individuals who have impacted your Christian life for good?

Kathy, Mom & Dad, Annette

DAY 5

Do not be anxious about anything, but in everything, by prayer and petition, with thanksgiving, present your requests to God.

Philippians 4:6

Therefore I tell you, do not worry about your life, what you will eat or drink; or about your body, what you will wear. Is not life more important than food, and the body more important than clothes? Look at the birds of the air; they do not sow or reap or store away in barns, and yet your heavenly Father feeds them. Are you not much more valuable than they? Who of you by worrying can add a single hour to his life?

Matthew 6:25–27

When I am afraid, I will trust in you.

Psalm 56:3

Relax. Chill. Lighten up. Take a chill pill. Any of these terms sound familiar? We have an entire lingo devoted to the idea of reducing our level of stress. Stressors in our lives can range from schoolwork to peer pressure to family problems and beyond. The fact is, stress has always been around. Well, since Genesis 3 anyway. Prior to the fall of man, Adam and Eve enjoyed stress-free communion with the God of the universe.

Unfortunately, that didn't last long. Our sin nature rose to the surface when Adam and Eve disobeyed God and incurred his judgment—separation from God, along with a litany of uncomfortable scenarios such as painful childbirth, working by the sweat of our brow, and death.

From then on, stress moved in and became a permanent fixture. Rich people stress about how to spend; poor people stress about how to pay the rent; beautiful people stress about losing their beauty; ugly people stress about peer rejection. It makes ya kinda stressed out just thinking about all that stress!

But wait—don't escape to the safety of your room just yet! Researchers say that not addressing stress in our lives only serves to make it worse. Running from the situation can actually trigger a whole host of physical problems.

Since God is all-knowing, all-present, and all-powerful, then he already knows all about your suicidal friend, or your looming math test, or your parents' divorce. And he knows how much it stresses you out.

Philippians 4:6 says, "Do not be anxious about anything . . ." OK, and here's the really cool part in verse 7: "And the peace of God, which transcends all understanding, will guard your hearts and your minds in Christ Jesus."

Stress is real. And here to stay, unfortunately. The very first step toward dealing with it as a Christian is to bring it before God. He's waiting to bestow peace on your troubled soul. Because if anyone can help you chill out, it's him.

↑ Looking Up

What is your current stress level? (1 = low, 10 = high)

What is the biggest stress in your life right now?

What are some things you have tried to reduce your stress level?

DAY 6

To you, O Lord, I lift up my soul; in you I trust, O my God. Do not let me be put to shame, nor let my enemies triumph over me. No one whose hope is in you will ever be put to shame, but they will be put to shame who are treacherous without excuse.

Psalm 25:1–3

For who is God besides the Lᴏʀᴅ? And who is the Rock except our God? It is
God who arms me with strength and makes my way perfect.

2 Samuel 22:32–33

And the God of all grace, who called you to his eternal glory in Christ, after you
have suffered a little while, will himself restore you and make you strong, firm
and steadfast.

1 Peter 5:10

It's nearly impossible to hide your smoking from your parents. Your
mom is always home, so smoking at home is impossible. Your dad has
the nose of a St. Bernard, and covering the smell is impossible. But
with the stress of school and your parents' strained marriage, smoking
is the one thing that calms you. One cigarette and you feel better. Your
parents would be angry if they found out you smoked, and you'd like
to find another way to handle your stress. The one person you feel you
can talk to is Martha, your youth pastor's wife.

You talk to Martha, but it doesn't help too much. Martha confides
in you that she used to smoke. She gave it up when her parents caught
her. "Your parents will probably find out, you know. And besides, God
knows what you're doing. He sees you."

You reply with a very tense, "You know, Martha, Santa and God are
not the same. I don't believe that God watches us all the time. There
are some things that he can't keep track of. Santa is a myth, and God's
keeping track of every small thing we do is a myth too."

Inside, you know that what she's saying is true. Admitting that God
knows you smoke means that you really ought to quit. Quitting is too
difficult, and it's just easier to argue. You spend the rest of the time
with Martha arguing. It gets heated. She gets very upset and tells you
it's either "get real with God or live your life hiding from everyone."

It's ridiculous to think God can't see you. What's behind your in-
ability to admit that you can't hide your smoking from God?

Fear.

Fear of being fully discovered. Fear of God's frustration with you.
Fear of having to actually deal with the stress you feel.

It's the secret you don't want anyone to uncover.

What does the Bible say about fear?

What is another way you could approach Martha or your parents with this situation?

What would you say if the roles were reversed and you were Martha being approached with this problem?

DAY 7

For the LORD is righteous, he loves justice; upright men will see his face.

Psalm 11:7

We know also that the Son of God has come and has given us understanding, so that we may know him who is true. And we are in him who is true—even in his Son Jesus Christ. He is the true God and eternal life.

1 John 5:20

Blessed are the pure in heart, for they will see God.

Matthew 5:8

Imagining God being in your presence is a little freaky. I mean, when you start saying things like, "Me and God . . . we're tight. We hang out a lot." People begin thinking about you like you're either super pious or a little wacko. Being honest with God falls into that same category. If you're vulnerable about your honesty with God, you begin to be uncomfortable to be around. After all, being honest with God means that you're taking steps to totally surrender everything in your life—from the really ugly stuff to the easy-to-reveal stuff.

If you're ready for this step and willing to do something a little tough, do this:

Go get a pair of sunglasses. Think of these sunglasses as being the eyes of God. When you put on these glasses, you're able to see the things in your life from his perspective. It's like he is looking at your life when you wear the glasses.

Put on the glasses and go to your room. Look around your bedroom and imagine that you're God, evaluating the kind of things you've got in your room. Imagine that you're discussing with God the things he is seeing. What things in your room would God question you about? What things in your room would he be displeased with? As you're evaluating your room, you might want to keep a list of the things you find questionable.

Next, go to your bathroom with the sunglasses on. Look over the room—is there anything God would be displeased with?

Go to a place where you keep private things. This could be your backpack, school locker, under your bed, etc. Anywhere you keep things you don't want others to see. Imagine God is seeing these places for the first time. Is he totally pleased? Anything he's upset about?

Here's a truth: we rarely live our lives believing that God really sees everything we do. With that in mind, what things in your life do you want to keep hidden from God? What do you think he would say about your private stash of stuff?

↑ Looking Up

What have you learned about being honest with God from this activity?

Using what you've learned from this illustration, how would you explain to your best friend the importance of being honest with God?

How can you apply what you've learned and the truth you've discovered from Scripture about this topic?

WHY SHOULD I BE HONEST WITH OTHERS?

DAY 1

The LORD detests lying lips, but he delights in men who are truthful.

Proverbs 12:22

Be very careful, then, how you live—not as unwise but as wise, making the most of every opportunity, because the days are evil. Therefore do not be foolish, but understand what the Lord's will is.

Ephesians 5:15–17

See how I love your precepts; preserve my life, O LORD, according to your love. All your words are true; all your righteous laws are eternal.

Psalm 119:159–60

You've probably heard all the old clichés:

"Honesty is the best policy"

"He's as honest as the day is long"

"God's honest truth"

"To be honest with you . . ."

Maybe you've read Revelation 21:8, where liars are eternally doomed to the fiery pit of hell.

You've been taught you're not supposed to lie about anything. So you don't . . . do you? When your parents ask you to tell them the truth, you do because you know it's the right thing to do. Then a teacher asks you to be honest with him about your homework, and you tell him.

That's not the kind of honesty we're talking about this week. There's another kind of honesty that goes beyond telling the truth. It's called being authentic, genuine, *real*.

How real are you with others? When they ask you how you're feeling, do you tell them? When a friend is messing up their life, do you tell them? When confronted by a non-Christian about your beliefs, do you give a vague answer and then simply walk away?

It's not always easy being genuine with others. Being that honest with people takes guts, and it requires an openness that few naturally possess. Think about it this way: when we choose not to help a friend understand that he's made a mistake, or when we choose not to tell a loved one the truth about God, that's being dishonest too. We don't have to tell a lie in order to be lying to someone. In fact, sometimes we don't have to say anything.

Below, write four things you have difficulty being honest about with others.

- _My past_
- _____
- _____
- _____

Not being honest with others damages relationships. We can seriously ruin our relationship with our parents and our best friends when we lie or choose not to tell them how we honestly feel.

(Warning: Be aware that revealing truth to others can also be risky. If you find yourself in a confrontational situation, be sure to look to the Scriptures for wisdom and to God for strength. And don't ever put yourself in a potentially dangerous arena without first consulting your parents or another adult whom you trust.)

↑ Looking Up

How is it possible to lie to someone while not saying a word?

Why does God desire honesty from us?

To whom do you turn when you need to share something in private? Who turns to you?

DAY 2

That is why, for Christ's sake, I delight in weaknesses, in insults, in hardships, in persecutions, in difficulties. For when I am weak, then I am strong.

2 Corinthians 12:10

LORD, who may dwell in your sanctuary? Who may live on your holy hill? He whose walk is blameless and who does what is righteous, who speaks the truth from his heart and has no slander on his tongue, who does his neighbor no wrong and casts no slur on his fellowman.

Psalm 15:1–3

These are the things you are to do: Speak the truth to each other, and render true and sound judgment in your courts.

Zechariah 8:16

Ever been to a slumber party and played the game Truth or Dare? Overnighters in my day were never complete without a lengthy rendition of this timeless treasure. I'm not sure exactly why we played; all participants were guaranteed to make fools of themselves, either by words or actions.

I almost always chose actions. I found a dare much less daunting than a verbal foray in the truth. Why? Because telling the truth was a lot harder than, say, running around the backyard in my pajamas or filling up the cat's food dish with whipped cream. In a word, it was much less *vulnerable*.

Being vulnerable means willingly opening yourself up for the possibility of being hurt, embarrassed, or attacked. Sounds fun, huh? It definitely is not a natural action. As humans, our natural tendency is to protect ourselves from external forces that could cause us pain.

Being honest with others includes an element of vulnerability. It opens up the potential for rejection. But it also opens up the potential for growth, for healing, and for deliverance.

Too often, as Christians, we hide our mistakes and problems from the outside world, thinking we're doing God some kind of a favor.

"What if they knew all my failings?" you may ask. "They won't want to be a Christian if they see how hard my life is and how often I've screwed up."

Not true, my friend. The Bible makes no bones about the fact that our lives will be riddled with problems, even after we become believers. It is not a perfect life or perfect decisions that draw others to the Lord—it's our response to external troubles and our own blunders that sets us apart from the rest of humanity.

Don't believe me? Check out these individuals in Scripture:

David—2 Samuel 22
Peter—1 Peter 1:3–9
Paul—Romans 7:15–20, 24–25

All three of these men were fallible. All made mistakes. All made a huge impact for God because of their willingness to be real, to be vulnerable, to be honest with others about their problems. This week saturate yourself with God's Holy Word. Take a step of faith and be completely honest with others around you. Take a deep breath and go forth in truth. I dare ya.

↑ Looking Up

What are some of the troubles of life that have taken you by surprise?

What is it that keeps you from being honest and vulnerable with others?

How does it make you feel when someone you trust and admire lies to you?

DAY 3

Love does not delight in evil but rejoices with the truth.

1 Corinthians 13:6

Then we will no longer be infants, tossed back and forth by the waves, and blown here and there by every wind of teaching and by the cunning and craftiness of men in their deceitful scheming. Instead, speaking the truth in love, we will in all things grow up into him who is the Head, that is Christ.

Ephesians 4:14–15

Therefore each of you must put off falsehood and speak truthfully to his neighbor, for we are all members of one body.

Ephesians 4:25

Pssst! Can you keep a secret?

It depends, of course, on your trustworthiness. A good secret keeper is trustworthy. When we entrust someone with a secret, we expect that the other person will not turn around and harm us with the secret that we confided.

Good friends, those who are trustworthy, are also those who hold you accountable to the truth that you profess. They keep you to your word. They do something when they notice you crossing a line you vowed never to cross. A good friend speaks the truth in love.

Being accountable to someone else means that we've made a promise and we'd like our friend to hold us to it. It's too easy to back away from something difficult when we face it alone. However, when we know our best friend is there beside us, holding us accountable, we somehow find the strength and courage to do the right thing.

When a friend asks you to hold him accountable, he wants you to be honest with him, no matter how hard it could be. He trusts you as his friend because you are reliable, steadfast, dependable, consistent, honest.

In order to keep your friend accountable, in regard to spiritual matters, you must first take the time to familiarize yourself with the Scriptures, with Truth. We're not talking about judging others; the emphasis here is that a believer has made a promise and then has come to you for backup.

I love old cops-and-robbers shows. Television scripts never seemed complete without a two-man team of cops going after the bad guys. And they never needed backup! Why? Because they knew they could handle it themselves—they were invincible!

We, however, are not invincible. We need backup—big time. Unlike those Hollywood police officers in the '70s, there is no way we can battle enemies and temptations alone. Thankfully, God has equipped us with several weapons of defense:

His Word—aka the Bible, the Scriptures

His Holy Spirit—aka the Comforter, the Counselor

His church—aka the body of believers, accountability backup

As a member of God's accountability backup, be encouraged to stand up and speak the truth in love with your fellow believers. If you have earned their friendship and trust, you have earned the right to be honest with them, especially if they've made some unhealthy decisions. Hopefully, your friends will realize that you are motivated by your concern for their well-being.

It's true. Some may turn away from you—hey, the truth can hurt at times! But more than likely, your friends will thank you in the end.

↑ Looking Up

Name some people who have earned your trust.

Why is it important to have an accountability backup?

What are some areas in your life where you need to have some accountability?

DAY 4

A truthful witness gives honest testimony, but a false witness tells lies.

Proverbs 12:17

But you will receive power when the Holy Spirit comes on you; and you will be my witnesses in Jerusalem, and in all Judea and Samaria, and to the ends of the earth.

Acts 1:8

I have seen and I testify that this is the Son of God.

John 1:34

"Order in the court! All rise. The Honorable Judge Judy presiding." Hmm, doesn't sound quite right, does it? How about "The infamous Judge Judy presiding"?

Courtrooms have been the subject of numerous television programs over the years. Here are a few you (or your parents) may recognize: *Perry Mason, Matlock, Law & Order, Murder One, Ally McBeal, JAG, Judging Amy, The Practice, Boston Legal, The People's Court.*

Law, mysteries, justice. All of these elements combine to form some of the most compelling television programs in history—especially for those of us who love courtroom scenes. What are the elements of a good courtroom setting?

1. Judge
2. Jury
3. Lawyers
4. Defendant
5. Witnesses

In a court case, the judge and jury listen to the evidence presented by the lawyers on behalf of the defendant. While the evidence is vital to the defense, it is the testimonies of witnesses that are critical to the outcome of the trial. The importance of documenting the details of witnesses can sometimes draw trials out over a period of weeks or even months. While a court proceeding is a lengthy and somewhat laborious process, it is the testimony of the witnesses that draws spectators to the edge of their seats. It would be a grave mistake to underestimate the power of a good witness.

And for any eyewitness to a crime, there exists a moral responsibility to proclaim the truth of what was seen and heard. If the witness refused to tell his or her side of the story, would it make the truth less true? Of course not. As a witness, reporting the facts you have seen helps spread that truth to others, such as the lawyers, jury, and judge.

See where I'm going yet? We as believers, as witnesses to the workings of the Holy Spirit of God, are morally compelled to share that truth with others. Whether or not we choose to share with others doesn't make the facts any more or less true. But our truth-telling, our testimony, does bring the spectators to the edge of their seats. There is nothing more compelling than the truth of Jesus Christ and his salvation to anyone who believes.

So, do you swear to tell the truth, the whole truth, and nothing but the truth, so help you God?

Good. All rise!

↑ Looking Up

What makes a person a good witness to a crime?

Why would God use us to share his truth with others?

Who is someone you'd like to share your testimony with this week?

DAY 5

The god of this age has blinded the minds of unbelievers, so that they cannot see the light of the gospel of the glory of Christ, who is the image of God.

2 Corinthians 4:4

Be self-controlled and alert. Your enemy the devil prowls around like a roaring lion looking for someone to devour. Resist him, standing firm in the faith, because you know that your brothers throughout the world are undergoing the same kind of sufferings.

1 Peter 5:8–9

"In your anger do not sin": Do not let the sun go down while you are still angry, and do not give the devil a foothold.

Ephesians 4:26–27

Ever heard the saying, "The devil made me do it"? It's most often used to explain some kind of mistake or goof up. Blaming it on the devil tends to lighten the mood and elicit a snicker or two from passersby. Why? Because most people picture the devil sprouting horns, wearing bright red spandex, and wielding a forked spear.

It's kinda hard to take him seriously in that light. And Satan loves it when we downplay his existence and his power. When we're chuckling about his red pajamas, then we're not exactly working to protect our hearts and minds from his influence.

As believers, we have the Spirit of God living inside us. That means we have access to his divine protection 24/7. Unfortunately, we don't always utilize this protection. We become lazy. We become apathetic. We become . . . unguarded.

Pretend you're going on a white-water rafting trip. You diligently pack all the necessary equipment but choose not to wear your life jacket. A foolish move, but you know in a pinch you can grab it at the last minute.

Your best friend is going on the same trip—without any equipment at all. But you let her come along, even though she's completely unprepared for the dangers posed by the river. After all, you tell yourself, it's her choice.

While you have the necessary protection at your fingertips, in an emergency you are both equally subject to the elements. The raging torrents around you won't wait for you to grab your life jacket; its power will pull you downward. And your unsuspecting friend will have no chance either.

Not being honest about God's lone ability to save your friend from Satan is like subjecting both you and your friend to the dangers of a tempestuous river. You would (I hope!) never dream of allowing your friend to make such a decision—at least not without providing her with relevant information about the trip. You would explain not just the excitement but also the dangers involved. You would inform because you care.

Not wearing your own life jacket and, instead, relying on your own strength against the forces of nature is like trying to battle Satan on your own. A foolish move, one the Bible clearly warns against: "Put on the full armor of God so that you can take your stand against the devil's schemes" (Ephesians 6:11).

Let's be honest—with our friends and ourselves. The devil is real, and only by the power of God can we stand against him. We need to inform those around us, not because we're judging them, but because we care.

↑ Looking Up

How does Hollywood portray Satan?

How does the Bible portray Satan?

How is it a victory for the devil when we're afraid to tell our friends how to be prepared against his schemes?

DAY 6

The righteous hate what is false, but the wicked bring shame and disgrace.

Proverbs 13:5

He who walks with the wise grows wise, but a companion of fools suffers harm.

Proverbs 13:20

A false witness will perish, and whoever listens to him will be destroyed forever.

Proverbs 21:28

Al's ability to spin a good story is known throughout your school. You've been Al's friend and biggest champion for years. Most people don't need a champion, but because of Al's weird and wild stories, he's needed someone in his corner. People don't take Al seriously, and it's really his own fault. Recently, Al has been spreading some pretty strange stories. Here's a rundown of a few of them.

There was the story about how his dad had gotten a promotion. The promotion meant that his dad's income would double, they'd be moving to a huge new home, and they'd probably go on a big, expensive family vacation to Europe to celebrate. When the vacation didn't happen, Al blamed it on his family being sick. No one really believes that his dad got the promotion or that he was moving anytime soon.

Al's mom supposedly "had cancer" and things weren't looking good. He augmented this story by acting depressed and crying all the time. The story was shot down when Al's mom appeared at the school play looking very healthy. One kid went up to her and asked about her cancer. Al's mom acted confused.

The story that had everyone talking was Al's announcement about winning a regional star-search contest. Since Al was on the school choral quartet, this wasn't totally impossible. Al announced to everyone that he had traveled to a city a few hours away, had competed in a talent contest, and had won. The win meant that he'd be going to a national contest that would be televised and could win him a $100,000 prize.

Everyone was talking about this, and it actually made Al more popular and more talked about in school. The story worked until someone realized that Al had been at the school basketball game on the same night he said the talent contest was held. When people began asking Al about how he had been at the school and the contest at the same time, he couldn't give a good explanation.

Al, your friend for years, has told enough untrue stories. It's been bugging you, and you feel like you need to talk to him about what he's been saying.

Who really cares if Al tells the truth or not? Why does it matter that Al constantly stretches the truth or tells flat-out lies?

↑ Looking Up

What are some ways you could approach Al with the truth?

How might Al react to being confronted with the truth?

If you were Al, how might you react?

How is Al's habit of lying affecting you, his friend?

DAY 7

Do not withhold your mercy from me, O LORD; may your love and your truth always protect me.

Psalm 40:11

The Word became flesh and made his dwelling among us. We have seen his glory, the glory of the One and Only, who came from the Father, full of grace and truth.

John 1:14

Truthful lips endure forever, but a lying tongue lasts only a moment.

Proverbs 12:19

Honesty is an interesting word. Think about its meaning; ideas like *vulnerability*, *truthfulness*, and *transparency* might come to mind. Is it difficult for you to be honest? Do you have difficulty being real with people? Take today to learn more about honesty.

Get a sheet of paper and write the word *liar* on it. At a time during the day when you'll interact with the most people (like at school or at church), tape the paper to your chest for one hour. More than likely people will notice you're wearing the paper. Once they've gotten over their initial surprise, they may ask you about it. Before you explain that you read the idea in a silly devotional book, ask them the following two questions:

"What does it mean to be honest?"

"What would it take for us to be honest with each other?"

Maybe they'll give you an answer, maybe not. Either way, explain to them that you're learning more about what it means to be honest with people around you, like with your friends and your parents. Make sure you write down their answers so you can read them later.

When you've worn the word for about an hour, take it off, find a place where you can concentrate, and look over the list of things you wrote down for each question. Read over the responses. What are your reactions to what you wrote down? What did you learn from the responses? How did it feel wearing "liar" for an hour? Was it uncomfortable?

You know what's true about lying and honesty—you can do both in secret. You could lie to people your whole life, and you might not get caught. You could also be honest 100 percent of your life, and no one might ever stop and say, "Man, you've got to be the most honest person in the world." Truth is, lying is often difficult to detect, and honesty is often not noticed or rewarded.

That makes both lying and honesty a choice—not of reward or punishment, but of inner character. This is about who you are. Whether or not people notice it, you're a liar if you spend your life lying, and you'll eventually wear that title like a stupid sign. If you spend your life being honest and real with those around you, you might not be rewarded, but your integrity and realness will affect everyone you meet.

↑ Looking Up

What have you learned from this activity about being honest with others?

Using what you've learned from this illustration, how would you explain the importance of being honest with others to your best friend?

How can you apply what you've learned and the truth you've discovered from Scripture about this topic?

WHY SHOULD I BE HONEST WITH MYSELF?

DAY 1

Hear my cry, O God; listen to my prayer.

Psalm 61:1

I pray also that the eyes of your heart may be enlightened in order that you may know the hope to which he has called you, the riches of his glorious inheritance in the saints, and his incomparably great power for us who believe. That power is like the working of his mighty strength, which he exerted in Christ when he raised him from the dead and seated him at his right hand in the heavenly realms.

Ephesians 1:18–20

He who ignores discipline comes to poverty and shame, but whoever heeds correction is honored.

Proverbs 13:18

We've already addressed the issue of lying to others and lying to God. This week we'll tackle the sticky subject of lying to ourselves and the damage we can unknowingly trigger.

Psychologists will tell you that not being honest with yourself can cause emotional problems that can eventually lead to depression or even death. Ignore a mental problem and you could end up talking to a padded wall.

The same goes for your spirit. If you're not honest with yourself, you can hinder your walk with God. A damaged spirit, one in need of attention, is just as debilitating as any physical injury.

So, stop for a sec and consider some things about which you've been lying to yourself. Here are a few ideas to consider if you're having trouble pinpointing some specifics:

What are some of your strengths and weaknesses? Everyone's got 'em. You, of all people, should know intimately the areas in which you struggle.

Is there anyone you've emotionally pushed away from or hurt recently?

How does your public personality match up with your private personality?

Has someone else hurt you? Are you willing to deal with that pain?

If you're still not able to complete this section objectively, have your parents or someone else you trust help you answer the questions.

- _____

- _____

- _____

- _____

What keeps you from being honest with yourself? What type of barricades have you set up in order to protect yourself from the truth? Write down four honesty roadblocks on the lines below. We will be dealing with these later in the week, so don't worry if you don't completely understand how these work.

- _____

- _____

- _____

- _____

↑ Looking Up

Why is it sometimes easier to lie to ourselves rather than face the truth?

Can you think of someone you trust who can help keep you accountable in your pursuit of honesty?

Why is it important to seek the truth in all things?

DAY 2

My mouth speaks what is true, for my lips detest wickedness.

Proverbs 8:7

But grow in the grace and knowledge of our Lord and Savior Jesus Christ. To him be glory both now and forever! Amen.

2 Peter 3:18

And when the men of that place recognized Jesus, they sent word to all the surrounding country. People brought all their sick to him and begged him to let the sick just touch the edge of his cloak, and all who touched him were healed.

Matthew 14:35–36

"Do you want to get well?"

In the fifth chapter of the book of John, Jesus asked this question of a man who had been an invalid for thirty-eight years. The Bible tells us that Jesus had found the man lying in front of the pool of Bethesda, a pool many thought to contain healing powers. However, the healing powers were only available if you actually got in the water.

The fact that the man was stationed near a source of healing showed his true desire for wellness; however, he was only *near* it, not *in* it. Did he really want to be well? Or was he a little fearful of the unknown, of being healed? Jesus asked a legitimate question, one that applies to you too.

There's something comforting in familiarity. Fear of the unknown often feels much more threatening than enduring that which we've come to accept, unhealthy as that may be.

Being honest about some things that are in need of a spiritual physician is not for the faint of heart. When God performs surgery on our hearts, he sometimes uses very little anesthetic, and he brandishes a blade that strikes strong and true.

But he is also very precise. God only cuts where it is absolutely necessary. He allows us to feel the pain in healing so that we rely completely on him for our recovery, and so we are strengthened for the next trial.

It takes guts to step out in faith. It takes courage to be willing to walk away from the comfort of familiarity. It takes nerve to ask for healing.

My question for you is this: do you *want* to get well?

↑ Looking Up

In what ways is our culture spiritually unhealthy?

Can you think of a time when you chose the familiar instead of the unknown?

What first step can you take toward being honest with yourself?

DAY 3

[Jesus] also told them this parable: "Can a blind man lead a blind man? Will they not both fall into a pit?"

Luke 6:39

[Jesus said,] While I am in the world, I am the light of the world.

John 9:5

You are my lamp, O LORD; the LORD turns my darkness into light.

2 Samuel 22:29

Ever played the game Blind Man's Bluff? How about Pin the Tail on the Donkey, or Marco Polo? Have you ever participated in a Trust Walk? What do all these games have in common? Darkness. Shadows. Blindness. Not to mention some good old-fashioned teasing from your friends.

All of these games show the disorientation that takes place when our eyes are covered. While in the safety of a party or in the company of friends, the disorientation is downright hilarious.

It's not too funny in the real world, when the blindness is spiritual and we're in the lead. Jesus asked one time, "Can a blind man lead a blind man? Will they not both fall into a pit?" (Luke 6:39).

When we fail to be honest with ourselves, we deny ourselves the illumination from the Keeper of the light, God. While we stumble around in the darkness, we thereby jeopardize those around us who may be following in our footsteps. Think no one's watching you? Think again.

How about that little brother or sister living down the hallway from you? Or the neighbor kid you occasionally babysit? There may be some kids at school who know you're a Christian and watch your interactions with others.

It's a big responsibility to be an example to others. One we should not take lightly. And one we shouldn't attempt without the Light, and without being honest with ourselves.

Look around this week and try to pinpoint those who may be following your lead in a spiritual Trust Walk. But keep your blindfold off—there are a lot of pits to avoid out there.

↑ Looking Up

Who are some individuals you have followed in your life for spiritual direction?

Why do you think God allows us to lead one another?

What are some of the different sensations we experience in the light of day versus the darkness of night?

DAY 4

Therefore, no one will be declared righteous in his sight by observing the law; rather, through the law we become conscious of sin.

Romans 3:20

What a wretched man I am! Who will rescue me from this body of death? Thanks be to God—through Jesus Christ our Lord!

Romans 7:24–25

But because of his great love for us, God, who is rich in mercy, made us alive with Christ even when we were dead in transgressions—it is by grace you have been saved.

Ephesians 2:4–5

Have you ever spaced out and given a gift with the price tag still attached? Ever received an expensive gift with the price tag still on? For some reason, when we've seen the cost of a pricey gift, it makes it seem even more special. "Wow!" we think to ourselves, "he spent *that* much on me?"

The opposite is true as well. We may be thrilled at first with that brand-new set of encyclopedias for Peruvian bird watching. But when we find out that Aunt Marge got them 85 percent off on clearance at the Bargain Barn, it just doesn't feel the same, does it?

We're nosy at heart. We want to know the cost, the price someone is willing to pay for us. It's as if we measure the level of their love by the expense. We really shouldn't think this way, but we often do.

The flip side to this is that it's a great way for us to think about God's love. Too often we take for granted what he's done for us. We become apathetic and numb to the amazement of grace. That's because we've become numb to the dreadfulness of sin.

And (you guessed it) that's where being honest with ourselves comes in. Honest in terms of our own corruption. Before you start beating yourself up about that time in kindergarten when you lied to your brother about eating his chocolate bar, you need to see the point to all this. The reason for seeing the ugliness of sin is not just to feel bad or to bash ourselves against the rocks of regret. It's to see how truly honored we are with the gift of God's grace.

I sometimes confuse *mercy* and *grace*. Let's get some definitions straightened out. When someone extends mercy to us, they are not giving us something bad we deserve—punishment. A judge can extend mercy to a prisoner. Grace is something good we don't deserve. It is an unearned gift given without strings attached.

When we are honest with ourselves, we see the sin in our lives for what it really is. Once we've truly perceived it for what it is and what it cost Jesus on the cross, we can finally recognize and appreciate the gift of grace God offers to us. It's the comparison between the two (sin versus grace) that reveals the incredible price that Jesus paid for us on the cross.

And you know what, that makes you pretty special. God spent everything he had just for you.

↑ Looking Up

Of all the gifts you've ever received, which one was your favorite?

What made that specific gift so meaningful to you?

Describe why God's grace is such an amazing gift for you.

DAY 5

The sacrifices of God are a broken spirit; a broken and contrite heart, O God, you will not despise.

Psalm 51:17

Therefore, I urge you, brothers, in view of God's mercy, to offer your bodies as living sacrifices, holy and pleasing to God—this is your spiritual act of worship.

Romans 12:1

He has showed you, O man, what is good. And what does the LORD require of you? To act justly and to love mercy and to walk humbly with your God.

Micah 6:8

I'm learning how to play the guitar and I'll tell ya—my fingers are stinging like crazy! I had no idea how much it hurt to play the guitar. I've been watching guitarists my whole life, as they pick, strum, and . . . well, look cool; never once have I seen a guitarist look pained while playing (Jimi Hendrix doesn't count—I'm pretty sure it was the drugs and not the guitar strings).

I know, I know—no pain, no gain, right? Oh, how troublesome those four words are to me, pain avoider extraordinaire. I hate pain. Big surprise, I'm sure. But to be honest with you, as I look back on my life, that slogan is so true! The things of which I am the most proud, that I remember with such clarity, and that matter the most, are those that involved at least some measure of pain, of sacrifice:

Graduating from college

Getting married

Becoming a new parent

Writing a book about parenting

Parenting in general (are you seeing a trend here?)

All of these things involved pain, discomfort, sacrifice. Pain is really just the sacrifice of comfort, isn't it? And yet without sacrifice of self, life would be steeped in stagnancy, self-centeredness, and apathy to everything and everyone around us. And although I've had to sacrifice a lot over the years, I can't imagine how empty my life would be without the blessings I've listed above.

Being honest with yourself requires a measure of sacrifice because it means you are willing to confront something painful. It is this willingness that God sees as an act of submission to him, as an act of worship.

Only when we have denied ourselves and subjected ourselves to the scrutiny of honest reflection can we fully come before him in obedience. Romans 12:1 talks about offering ourselves up to God as living sacrifices.

In the Old Testament, sacrifices were only acceptable to God when they were pure, without blemish. Before you offer yourself to him, take a moment to be honest with him. Allow him to wash away your sins and clean you up inside so that you will be a pleasing sacrifice to him.

And although it may be a bit painful, you won't regret it. If our gifts to God came without a price, they wouldn't be worth much, would they?

Besides, no pain, no gain, right?

↑ Looking Up

What accomplishment of yours are you most proud of?

Did it involve a measure of pain, of sacrifice on your part?

Can you think of something you need to offer to God as a sacrifice today?

DAY 6

Finally, brothers, whatever is true, whatever is noble, whatever is right, whatever is pure, whatever is lovely, whatever is admirable—if anything is excellent or praiseworthy—think about such things.

Philippians 4:8

Show me your ways, O LORD, teach me your paths; guide me in your truth and teach me, for you are God my Savior, and my hope is in you all day long.

Psalm 25:4–5

This is the message we have heard from him and declare to you: God is light; in him there is no darkness at all. If we claim to have fellowship with him yet walk in the darkness, we lie and do not live by the truth. But if we walk in the light,

as he is in the light, we have fellowship with one another, and the blood of
Jesus, his Son, purifies us from all sin.

1 John 1:5–7

Bethany's dad, Frank, always invites her friends out for the weekly
family meal at the steakhouse. Frank is the kind of guy who's wonder-
fully awful to be around. Wonderful because, at first, Frank seems
very generous. But awful because he can also be mean, antagonistic,
and overly negative—especially to his family. Frank's need to always
be right and his desire to argue about everything makes him very difficult to be around.

Frank's favorite emotion is anger. He'll get angry about anything.
Even when he's happy, his happiness seems to come out in a kind of
angry tone.

However, the biggest problem facing Bethany's dad is his frequent
bouts of memory loss. Actually, his memory lapses are more a problem
for the family than they are for Frank. He forgets phone numbers; he
forgets where he put his checkbook; he forgets names, dates, appointments. He can have the same conversation with you five times and
forget he's ever talked with you.

Frank's forgetfulness mixed with his anger has created an interesting and ongoing problem. When Frank loses his keys or wallet, it's
someone else's fault, and he yells at whoever's fault he decides it is.
When someone has a conversation with him (and he forgets it), he
gets angry that other people are more informed about stuff than he is.
Frank's over-the-top anger and his forgetfulness are creating serious
discomfort for his family.

For months now, Frank has been having irregular heartbeats at least
once a week. The doctor has run several tests but can't find anything.
Recently, when the irregularity became more frequent, his doctor said
it was time to see a neurologist. The combination of the heart problems and forgetfulness are demonstrating that Frank has some serious
problems. Unfortunately Frank refuses to admit he has a problem and
says he doesn't have the money to get his heart checked out. Bethany
and her mom just want him to get help.

Why do you think Frank refuses to admit he has a medical
  problem?

What will happen to Frank if he continues to go without treatment?
  What will happen to his family?

How does dishonesty with yourself about a physical problem compare to dishonesty about a spiritual problem?

DAY 7

Do what is right and good in the LORD'S sight, so that it may go well with you
and you may go in and take over the good land that the LORD promised on
oath to your forefathers.

Deuteronomy 6:18

Blessed are those who wash their robes, that they may have the right to the tree
of life and may go through the gates into the city.

Revelation 22:14

Let their lying lips be silenced, for with pride and contempt they speak arro-
gantly against the righteous.

Psalm 31:18

Do you lie to yourself? Do you ever say, "This will never happen" when
you know it probably will? Do you say, "I'll never" when you know you
probably will? Do you ever say, "I didn't" when you know you did?

I can already hear you say, "Me? I lie to myself?" I can hear the disbelief in your voice too. So, before you start calling *me* a liar and say
I'm outta my mind, do this and explore what you don't know about
yourself: Find five people who know you and love you enough to be
completely honest with you. Make sure these are people who really

care about you. (Beware of anyone who likes tearing others down; they might enjoy this too much.) Ask them the following questions:

Tell me three good things about me.

What areas of my life encourage you?

Tell me something you don't think I know about myself.

Tell me one way I could improve who I am.

Write their answers down so you can read them later. When you've had the chance to ask five people and after you've recorded their answers, find a place where you can be alone and evaluate everything you've heard.

First, read through their answers. Second, reflect on the general things you remember from your conversations. Third, answer this question: what things about you have you not been honest about?

As you evaluate and reflect, remember this: God made you and has designed you for this planet to glorify him. He uses people and experiences to continue to shape you into his image and likeness. When we're not honest with ourselves or when we lie to ourselves about who we are or what we've done, it is as if we're knowingly taking steps away from what God designed us to be. Not being honest with ourselves confuses who we're supposed to be. And, in the end, when we're not honest with ourselves, we can really ruin who we could have been.

↑ Looking Up

What have you learned about being honest with yourself from this activity?

Using what you've learned from this illustration, how would you explain the importance of being honest with yourself to your best friend?

How can you apply what you've learned, and the truth you've discovered from Scripture about this topic?

WHY SHOULD I BE
HUMBLE?

DAY 1

Therefore, whoever humbles himself like this child is the greatest in the kingdom of heaven.

Matthew 18:4

Therefore, as God's chosen people, holy and dearly loved, clothe yourselves with compassion, kindness, humility, gentleness and patience. Bear with each other and forgive whatever grievances you may have against one another. Forgive as the Lord forgave you. And over all these virtues put on love, which binds them all together in perfect unity.

Colossians 3:12–14

Seek the LORD, all you humble of the land, you who do what he commands. Seek righteousness, seek humility; perhaps you will be sheltered on the day of the LORD's anger.

Zephaniah 2:3

You stand at attention. This is the way it's supposed to be.

"And another thing, you worthless piece of human trash. You will listen to everything I say. You will obey every little thing I command you to do."

Pride. You're filled with pride. Honored to be treated with such disdain.

"Stand at ATTENTION! When I hit you, you WILL respond with a 'thank you, sir!'"

Your parents would be proud. You think, *If this kind of treatment was good enough for Jesus, it's good enough for me. I deserve this.*

Slowly and with great thought, Commander Callous walks around you. Checking and rechecking. Looking for your mistakes. Searching for ways to humiliate you. To make you more humble. With each step, you're thankful to be so closely associated with Christ. Each put-down makes you proud to be a believer. Each slap helps you realize your inferior position.

God is proud of the way you're facing this.

Whoa. Hold on; wait just a minute. Back up the truck, Chuck.

Something about this scenario is a little disturbing. OK, *very* disturbing.

Too often we think that being humble is the same as welcoming abuse and humiliation. We think that being humble means that we're mistreated and beaten up. We believe that the best way for a believer to follow Jesus is to be attacked and disgraced—all for the glory of God.

Not so, my friend. This week we're going to find out the true meaning of humility and why we want to seek after this all-important virtue. But first, let's look at your definition of humility. Write it down and check back on Day 5 to see if you were right.

_____

_____

_____

_____

↑ Looking Up

Why do you think God values humility?

How does the world view humility?

What is the difference between humility and humiliation?

DAY 2

I am the LORD; that is my name! I will not give my glory to another or my praise to idols.

Isaiah 42:8

O LORD, our Lord, how majestic is your name in all the earth! You have set your glory above the heavens.

Psalm 8:1

Humble yourselves before the Lord, and he will lift you up.

James 4:10

Glory. A familiar word that may be a little difficult to define. Obsessive pursuit of glory has rendered more than one world leader impotent, immobile, irrelevant, and often imprisoned. Here's the official definition: having great honor, fame, splendor, adoration.

Honor and fame aren't necessarily the problem. We cross over the line, however, when we seek splendor and adoration, when we try to steal God's glory. Why? Because God's glory is his own. Period. He alone deserves adoration.

From the very beginning, God's glory has been sought after. Satan, Adam and Eve, the people of Babel. When created beings try to usurp their Creator, they lose every time. The results are always punishment, isolation, and death.

Ahh, but when we humble ourselves before the Lord, giving glory to him, he is honored and we are lifted up by the Glorious One. There is no shame in acknowledging your position in relationship to God. Rather, there is honor, the honor granted by God.

So to recap: When we strive for glory and adoration, we suffer God's wrath and his judgment. When we give God honor, praise, and glory for who he is, he lifts us up and grants us honor as his children.

Sounds like a no-brainer, doesn't it? Rebellion and judgment versus obedience and honor. Take some time this week to consider ways you can honor your Creator, to give him glory, to give him your adoration.

↑ Looking Up

Why does the world balk at giving glory to God?

Can you think of a time when you tried to take the credit, the glory, from God?

What are some things you can thank him for and give him glory for right now?

DAY 3

The LORD's curse is on the house of the wicked, but he blesses the home of the righteous. He mocks proud mockers but gives grace to the humble.

Proverbs 3:33–34

Before his downfall a man's heart is proud, but humility comes before honor.

Proverbs 18:12

An argument started among the disciples as to which of them would be the greatest. Jesus, knowing their thoughts, took a little child and had him stand beside him. Then he said to them, "Whoever welcomes this little child in my name welcomes me; and whoever welcomes me welcomes the one who sent me. For he who is least among you all—he is the greatest."

Luke 9:46–48

Ever heard of the pecking order? Or being henpecked?

We're the proud owners of chickens at our house, and we've learned a few things about our fowl friends in the last few years. First of all, they're stinky. Really stinky. And they're not too bright either.

Other than that, they're great. Especially when they're only a couple of days old. They're so soft and fluffy (and relatively poop-free). But as they lose their baby feathers and they begin to mature, the inevitable happens—they vie for position. They peck at each other, establishing their all-important place in the poultry procession.

Some are naturally more aggressive than others; still others have the weight thing going for them—they're simply bigger than everyone else—and they use it to their full advantage.

The funny thing is that it really doesn't mean much. When the dust has settled, they're all just chickens. They all get fed and watered by their benevolent farmer (me!); they all get the same treatment, the same medicines, and the same calcium supplements. Their supposed superiority is only acknowledged by the four remaining chickens in a dog kennel in our backyard.

In light of that, it's ridiculous and somewhat embarrassing to watch the head of the henhouse strut her stuff; to watch her get so full of herself, all for . . . nothing. No recognition, no credit, no admiration, no respect.

My chickens remind me of people.

I know, I know, we're not chickens. But in a way, we're a lot like them. Compared to the greatness of God, we are mere chickens living in a coop surrounded by other chickens and wading through our own messes. Some of us are more aggressive than others; some are just plain bigger—and we use it to our full advantage.

But God desires us to see ourselves as equals to our fellow chickens—er, I mean, people. When we finally see ourselves for who we are in relation to the Father, our heavenly Farmer, suddenly all the henpecking seems meaningless, and a little embarrassing.

Having true humility means seeing your neighbor as an equally important member of the coop. It also prevents unnecessary vying for position that is ultimately meaningless. Humility allows us more time to seek after God and frees us from the pitfalls of the henhouse hierarchy, which, I've heard, isn't all it's cracked up to be anyway.

↑ Looking Up

What kinds of attributes or possessions make one great on earth?

What kinds of attributes make one great in heaven?

Why do you think we establish a pecking order?

DAY 4

Take my yoke upon you and learn from me, for I am gentle and humble in heart, and you will find rest for your souls.

Matthew 11:29

Do nothing out of selfish ambition or vain conceit, but in humility consider others better than yourselves. Each of you should look not only to your own interests, but also to the interests of others. Your attitude should be the same as that of Christ Jesus.

Philippians 2:3–5

And we, who with unveiled faces all reflect the Lord's glory, are being transformed into his likeness with ever-increasing glory, which comes from the Lord, who is the Spirit.

2 Corinthians 3:18

I don't particularly like walking through a house of mirrors. You know, the kind you might find at a carnival that stretches your image into all kinds of grotesque shapes. In walking a span of a measly twelve feet, your body style can range from toothpick tall to rhino rotund and everything in between. It's hardly complimentary—and to be truthful—a little disconcerting.

It's disturbing because our expectation when looking into a mirror is to see an accurate reflection of ourselves; however, with a house of mirrors, all of the images are distortions that completely misrepresent our true identity.

When I think of my prayer time, I wonder if Jesus sometimes feels like he's walking through a house of mirrors. As a believer whose body is a temple of the Holy Spirit, I am to mirror and reflect the actions and attitudes, the very person of Jesus Christ.

And yet, when he looks into my being, does he see himself stretched, squished, twisted into a warped representation of my own making? Does he see the dullness of pride where humility is supposed to glimmer?

What does he see when he looks into your being?

Stop for a moment and think about some ways you struggle with pride. Being prideful means you have accepted a warped image of your own importance; you consider yourself above others, and possibly above God.

As a believer, if you suffer from pride, your spiritual reflection is less than complimentary—in fact, it is downright repulsive. Be honest with the Lord about pride. Confess and allow him to forgive you. Watch in awe as he bends that distorted reflection back into one that mirrors his true image and identity.

What is the difference between good pride and being prideful?
How do you struggle in the area of pride?
Why is God concerned with our spiritual reflection?

DAY 5

Humility and the fear of the LORD bring wealth and honor and life.

Proverbs 22:4

Be completely humble and gentle; be patient, bearing with one another in love.

Ephesians 4:2

Who is wise and understanding among you? Let him show it by his good life, by deeds done in the humility that comes from wisdom.

James 3:13

Have you learned anything new about humility? Look back to see what you wrote on Day 1. Rewrite your definition based on your study from this week:

_____

_____

_____

_____

I'm a big fan of Spiderman. I've got a Spiderman keychain, a Spiderman mug, and several Spidey comic books. I've even been on the

Spiderman ride in Orlando, Florida, and—you guessed it—it's my all-time favorite ride.

I like all the other superheroes too. Superman seems nice enough, although sometimes I think he seems just a little *too* nice. Batman doesn't really have any superhero powers, which could be why he's so serious and down in the dumps all the time (I think a little counseling may actually be in order for Batman; the guy needs to *lighten up*). Wonder Woman looks too perfect; Robin is too . . . well . . . corny.

However, Spiderman has everything they lack: a really cool spidey suit, good sense of humor, a believable personality, and humility. He's just a really nice guy who sometimes makes mistakes, like the rest of us.

Spidey's creator, Stan Lee, once commented about the realness of Peter Parker, aka Spiderman:

> I think [Peter Parker] was very empathetic. Most of the young readers could identify with him because he had all the hang-ups that they did. . . . He'd be worried about acne or dandruff or an ingrown toenail, anything. . . . He makes mistakes and so forth. And again, I think that makes it easy for a reader to identify with him. And of course, that makes readers like him.[*]

Peter Parker is believable because he's not perfect—and because he doesn't pretend to be. As Christians, I think we undermine our efforts to witness for Christ when we feign perfection. When we ignore our faults, our mistakes, our vulnerabilities.

But when we are humble, when we can set aside our pride and admit the goofs we've made, people can identify with us. They will want to listen to us. Before you get caught in a web of pride fashioned out of your own self-importance, remember our friendly neighborhood Spiderman. And remember that God is the true Superhero; we're just here to point others to him.

[*] Stan Lee, CNN.com Entertainment, May 4, 2002, http://archives.cnn.com/2002/ SHOWBIZ/Movies/05/04/spiderman.stanlee.cnna/, accessed November 15, 2004.

How do you think others perceive you?

How do you wish they perceived you?

Why is it important to be real with people, not perfect?

DAY 6

Live in harmony with one another. Do not be proud, but be willing to associate with people of low position. Do not be conceited.

Romans 12:16

To fear the LORD is to hate evil; I hate pride and arrogance, evil behavior and perverse speech. Counsel and sound judgment are mine; I have understanding and power.

Proverbs 8:13–14

Pride goes before destruction, a haughty spirit before a fall.

Proverbs 16:18

Ben is good at football. Really, really good at football. He's been scouted by the state university and by a couple of pro teams. He's won every award the school has for sports. Coach loves Ben. He's Coach's "second son." But Coach can't stand Ben's arrogance. He loves that Ben helps win games, but he can't stand Ben's postgame, cocky attitude.

You've run into Ben at a party at a friend's house. The conversation turns quickly to football (because that's usually all Ben talks about).

"I'm done with it. Coach has been pushing me really hard. It's too much."

"I don't understand." You're not sure you heard Ben right—the music is a little loud, and you're *sure* Ben didn't just say he was quitting football.

"I'm done with football. Coach is riding me too much. He's been doing everything he can think of to make me look stupid. Last week he had me washing the team jerseys. I shouldn't have to wash their jerseys—I'm the quarterback! Coach says I'm too cocky. I'm too proud. He's doing this because he says it'll make me humble. He says the best players are humble."

"That doesn't sound too bad. How bad could it be? It sounds like he's just trying to make you a better player."

"Yeah, but sometimes he pushes too hard. He'll stand right by me as I'm working out in the gym and yell at me about how average I am, and how I need to work harder. Sometimes it's cool. But sometimes he just makes me feel stupid."

The music is too loud to continue the conversation. You don't feel like trying to yell some kind of helpful advice over the noise. What should you say to Ben? Yeah, he's always been a little too cocky, but he's not that bad. Does Coach know best? He seems to think the best way to make Ben a better player and take him down a few notches is to make him feel stupid. What do you think?

↑ Looking Up

What are some things about Ben that his coach is trying to change?

Do you agree with his methods? Why or why not?

How do you think God helps us to be humble?

DAY 7

Young men, in the same way be submissive to those who are older. All of you, clothe yourselves with humility toward one another.

1 Peter 5:5

"Rise in the presence of the aged, show respect for the elderly and revere your God. I am the LORD."

Leviticus 19:32

Honor your father and your mother, as the LORD your God has commanded you, so that you may live long and that it may go well with you in the land the LORD your God is giving you.

Deuteronomy 5:16

So often we think being humble means being someone's doormat. We think humility means letting others push us around, or not standing up for ourselves, or allowing someone to make fun of us. The fact is, being humble doesn't mean we're everyone's servant. To get a better idea of what it means to be humble, try the following exercise using some matches. Be sure to read through these instructions before getting started.

Two books of matches will work best for this. Make sure you are in a place where you can burn matches, and that you've got a safe place to lay several used ones that might still be hot. Observe the following things about the matches as they burn:

* Heat   * Time

For each of the following activities, you'll be asked to light a match, possibly several. When you light each match, let it burn until it's close to your finger, then blow it out. (NOTE: For the pyrotech-inclined—this is not a contest to see how close you can let the match come to burning you!)

Keep in mind the definition for *humble* that I've tweaked from Webster's official definition: "Having or showing a consciousness of one's defects; being aware of one's true nature, value, and importance."

OK, let's get started:

1. Think about some of your strengths or areas where you are gifted. Are you a musician? An artist? A jokester? A good friend? Everyone has something they excel in—what's yours? Burn a

match to thank God for the unique ways he has made you and for the particular gifts he has hardwired into your personality. Ask God to help you use those gifts to bring light to others.

2. Think of your weaknesses, the places you fail more often than you'd like. Everyone has areas to improve, and you're no different. Light a match as you ask God to burn away those things and make you more like him.

3. Think of an area where you are prideful and consider yourself superior to others. Pride has been around since the beginning of time, and if you think it hasn't touched your life, think again! As you burn another match, pray and ask God to help you be more humble in this area. Picture your pride being snuffed out by God as you blow out the match.

4. Think about a time when someone else treated you inferior, as less important than themselves. Remember how that felt. Light a match and ask God to help you forgive that person. Don't allow any anger or bitterness to continue to smolder; instead, ask God to reduce those thoughts and feelings to ashes.

Before you began, you had either a box of matches or a book of matches. Each match possessed the same value; in other words, no match was more important than the others. Being humble is being aware that you are neither more *nor less* valuable than others. In God's eyes, each soul is valued equally.

Every time a match is burned, both heat and time are involved. The *heat* helps us remember how brightly we can burn for God's glory; it also reminds us of how God can burn away the bad stuff in our hearts. The *time* it takes for a small match to burn out reminds us of our significance in relation to God. We are on earth for a short while, but God has always been and always will be. He has always existed—a mind-boggling reality. By possessing a realistic view of ourselves, one that acknowledges both our gifts and our weaknesses, we can be truly humble.

↑ Looking Up

What have you learned about being humble from this activity?

Using what you've learned from this illustration, how would you explain the importance of being humble to your best friend?

How can you apply what you've learned and the truth you've discovered from Scripture about this topic?

WHY SHOULD I SERVE OTHERS?

DAY 1

Jesus answered, "It is written: 'Worship the Lord your God and serve him only.'"

Luke 4:8

And now, O Israel, what does the LORD your God ask of you but to fear the LORD your God, to walk in all his ways, to love him, to serve the LORD your God with all your heart and with all your soul?

Deuteronomy 10:12

But as for me and my household, we will serve the LORD.

Joshua 24:15

How do you define service? Maybe it's

a waiter who honestly doesn't mind clearing your dishes after a
really messy meal . . .
a gas station attendant who fills up your tank, washes your windows,
and checks your oil—at no extra charge and with a smile . . .
a hotel bellhop who cheerfully hauls your baggage up to the thirty-
second floor and refuses the tip you offer him.

Honest-to-goodness service has become a lost art. Why? Because so often there are strings attached to public service. It's the old "You scratch my back, I'll scratch yours" mentality rearing its ugly head.

Good old Webster defines *service* as "work done for others." For others. Period. Without pay, bonuses, tips, favors, or remuneration of any kind. Service is giving without any thought to oneself.

Huh? I don't know about you, but that concept is pretty unfamiliar. I spend so much of my time taking care of myself that the "others" in my life inevitably get left behind. This week we're going to study the importance of reviving the principle of service to "others" in our lives and why it's so important in the life of a thriving Christian.

List some of the "others" in your life you would like to serve:

- _____
- _____
- _____
- _____
- _____

Unfortunately, most of us would like others to get their principle of service figured out. Because then they can serve *us*—right? We're sinful creatures who are bent on satisfying our own wants and desires. It is this sinful tendency that makes it so difficult to see past ourselves to the others around us whom God would have us serve.

Here's a classic example. One morning, my nine-year-old son came upstairs with a confused look on his face. "What's the matter?" I asked. With an expression of pure disbelief, he said, "There's no one downstairs serving breakfast!"

The kid knew how to serve himself breakfast, but that morning he thought the rest of us should have been serving him. And apparently the thought of putting others first—of getting breakfast out for the rest of the family—was as foreign to him as a bellhop refusing a hefty tip. Or a gas attendant going out of his way to provide free full service. Maybe you can relate; I know I can. Let's set aside our tip jar for a moment and take a look in the Scriptures to rediscover the lost art of service.

↑ Looking Up

When was the last time you served others without any thought of yourself?

Why do you think it's important to serve others?

Who are some people who have selflessly served you?

DAY 2

I tell you the truth, whatever you did for one of the least of these brothers of mine, you did for me.

Matthew 25:40

Whatever you do, work at it with all your heart, as working for the Lord, not for men.

Colossians 3:23

Serve wholeheartedly, as if you were serving the Lord, not men, because you know that the Lord will reward everyone for whatever good he does, whether he is slave or free.

Ephesians 6:7–8

You're going to have to serve somebody. Your parents may remember a song along those lines written by Bob Dylan in 1979.

Although we live in a three-dimensional world, there exists a spiritual world as well, comprised of Satan and his demons, God and his angels. Two sides only, which means if you're not serving one, you're serving the other.

Jesus says in Matthew that if we have done something selflessly for someone else, then we've done it unto him—we've served him. In his paraphrase *The Message*, Eugene Peterson renders Matthew 25:35–40 like this:

> I was hungry and you fed me,
> I was thirsty and you gave me a drink,
> I was homeless and you gave me a room,
> I was shivering and you gave me clothes,
> I was sick and you stopped to visit,
> I was in prison and you came to me.
> . . . I'm telling the solemn truth: Whenever you did one of these things to someone overlooked or ignored, that was me—you did it to me.

I don't have a death wish or anything, but I'm really looking forward to getting to heaven. Heaven—a place where there are no tears, no fears, no traffic, no dieting, no selfishness. But I'm mostly anticipating my entrance into eternity to hear the words from Jesus, "Well done, good and faithful servant."

Now, on my own, I know I will NEVER earn the right to hear those amazing words. Left to my own devices, I would spend my entire life serving myself, which translates in the spiritual realm as serving Satan. Serving Satan? How could a good person like me be serving Satan? Easily. All too easily, in fact.

Thankfully, Jesus left a legacy of selflessness behind, as well as his empowering Holy Spirit, to remind us to look around every now and again and tend to the needs of others. Every action we take serves someone. It might be ourselves (translation: Satan), it might be someone who is overlooked and ignored (translation: the Lord). The question to ask yourself is this: Who are *you* gonna serve?

↑ Looking Up

What are some ways you have served yourself in the past?

What are some ways you have served others?

Can you think of anyone who is ignored or overlooked in your life whom you could serve?

DAY 3

Suppose a brother or sister is without clothes and daily food. If one of you says to him, "Go, I wish you well; keep warm and well fed," but does nothing about his physical needs, what good is it? In the same way, faith by itself, if it is not accompanied by action, is dead.

James 2:15–17

A new command I give you: Love one another. As I have loved you, so you must love one another. By this all men will know that you are my disciples, if you love one another.

John 13:34–35

Be imitators of God, therefore, as dearly loved children and live a life of love, just as Christ loved us and gave himself up for us as a fragrant offering and sacrifice to God.

Ephesians 5:1–2

Trial by fire. Have you ever experienced a trial by fire? I have, many times: my first day of teaching; my first public speaking gig; taking my driver's license test—for the third time; coming home from the hospital with our first child. A trial by fire implies the testing of one's abilities under pressure. While being observed. By other people. Other people who can scrutinize, analyze, and criticize our efforts.

Being put to the test is not generally a pleasant occasion. But it is an educational one, both for the spectator and the participant. The scrutinizer learns by simple observation whether or not we are who we claim to be: a teacher, a speaker, a driver, a parent. If we don't measure up, our actions will eventually betray us.

Serving others is a type of trial by fire, although not as stressful as a driver's test! But we are tested and watched to see if our claim that we are a new creation in Christ is valid. Our actions are truly a reflection of our faith in Jesus Christ.

In *The Lord of the Rings*, the wizard, Gandalf, suspects that the magic ring held for so many years by Bilbo Baggins is the One Ring of power, which is relentlessly hunted by the evil Lord Sauron. This One Ring is so evil, and wields a power so great, it can destroy all of Middle-earth.

Upon examination, the Ring looks like any other gold ring; it is plain, smooth, cool to the touch. However, when exposed to fire, its real purpose is exposed as words appear on the inside of the Ring; these words are written in the language of Sauron, the Ring's lord and creator. It is the trial of fire that finally confirms the Ring's true nature.

As you serve God in obedience, you will be closely examined by others. At first glance, you may look like any other teenager. But just as the nature of Sauron's ring is inevitably revealed, so will your faith in Christ be revealed. The authenticity of God's transforming power will be seen in how you serve and care for others in the name of Jesus Christ.

Some questions you may want to ask yourself:

Am I serving with the empowerment of the Holy Spirit?
Am I merely doing good works through my own efforts?
Am I serving others at all?

Jesus said that all men would know we are his disciples by how we love one another. Think about that this week as you look for ways to serve others in love. Expect to be tested by the fire; it's the only way others can know our true nature.

Is it just me or is it getting a little warm in here?

↑ Looking Up

Can you think of someone whose true nature was revealed by their service to others?
What kinds of service to others reveal a genuine faith in Christ?
What do others see when they watch you?

DAY 4

For we are God's workmanship, created in Christ Jesus to do good works which God prepared in advance for us to do.

Ephesians 2:10

Dear friends, let us love one another, for love comes from God. Everyone who loves has been born of God and knows God.

1 John 4:7

Whoever wants to become great among you must be your servant, and whoever wants to be first must be your slave—just as the Son of Man did not come to be served, but to serve and to give his life as a ransom for many.

Matthew 20:26–28

Ever asked yourself the question, "What on earth am I here for?"

You're not alone. In 2002 and 2003, millions of Americans joined author Rick Warren in his quest for purpose by reading his bestseller, *The Purpose-Driven Life*. Thousands of churches nationwide participated in a forty-day adventure as they came together in pursuit of concrete answers to this question.

In *The Purpose-Driven Life*, Warren (pastor of one of the largest churches in the world, Saddleback Church in Lake Forest, California) outlines five answers to that question. Here are the "CliffsNotes":

1. You were planned for God's pleasure
2. You were formed for God's family
3. You were created to become like Christ
4. You were shaped for serving God
5. You were made for a mission*

OK, refresh your memory and take a look at number 4 again. Yep. You were shaped for serving God. And one of the main ways to serve God is to serve others. Don't take my word for it, though—or Rick Warren's. Open up your Bible and peruse the Gospels: Matthew, Mark, Luke, and John.

Every moment of Jesus's adult life was spent serving others. And although service to others is often less than glamorous, Jesus lovingly lent himself to caring for all kinds of people: lepers, widows, the impoverished, the unclean, the unrepentant, and the ungrateful.

The tough part about service is that it isn't always recognized or appreciated to the extent we want. In fact, it often goes undetected and unannounced. However, if we remember that we're serving others, not for worldly appreciation and acknowledgment, but out of our love for

* Rick Warren, *The Purpose-Driven Life* (Grand Rapids: Zondervan, 2002).

God and his purposes for us, then we can continue to serve, knowing that he sees. He cares. He is honored by our service.

So now that you know why you're here, what on earth are you going to do to serve others this week?

↑ Looking Up

What are some talents and abilities God has given you?

How could you use these to serve others?

What are some things that make it so difficult for us to reach out and serve others?

DAY 5

Whoever serves me must follow me; and where I am, my servant also will be. My Father will honor the one who serves me.

John 12:26

If anyone speaks, he should do it as one speaking the very words of God. If anyone serves, he should do it with the strength God provides, so that in all things, God may be praised through Jesus Christ. To him be the glory and the power for ever and ever. Amen.

1 Peter 4:11

Now that I, your Lord and Teacher, have washed your feet, you also should wash one another's feet.

John 13:14

Foot washing. Nasty business, that. Think about it: foot fungus, ingrown toenails, bunions. I had a pedicure once, and I made sure to clean my tootsies thoroughly before handing them over to the poor pedicure professional. During the process I kept apologizing for the condition of my feet. She was completely unfazed, though. "Oh my, you should see some of the feet I get in here!" Somewhat skeptical of her foot assessment, I made sure to give her a hefty tip before I shuffled out.

I was in a Bible study class a few years ago, and for my week to teach, I chose to focus on the passage in John 13, the foot washing. Being a "hands-on" kind of person, following the lesson I arranged the chairs in a circle and worked my way around the room, carefully washing each person's feet.

Some were shocked.

Others were embarrassed.

Many quietly cried.

And one flat out refused to let me touch her feet. She chose instead to skip out, leaving me without the privilege of blessing her, and her without the privilege of being blessed.

It was the ones who cried who touched me the most. I think they cried because they knew it was a nasty business but I chose to be obedient to Christ, to follow his example, to love them through the act of servitude. I think they cried because they knew that on my own I wouldn't come near their ingrown toenails and bunions—they knew it was Jesus living inside me, who prompted me to perform such a selfless act.

There are lots of different "foot washing" types of service out there. The kinds of service that make people take a second look and ask, "Why are you doing this?" My friend, that is the moment when you can introduce them to Jesus, Lover of the unlovely, Giver to the ungrateful, Friend to the friendless.

Acts of service are crucial in the life of a Christian. They honor God, they get our eyes off ourselves, they bless people, but more importantly, they draw people to Jesus Christ.

My life as a worker is the way I say "thank you" to God for His unspeakable salvation.

Oswald Chambers

Can you think of some "foot washing" services done for you by others?

How would you respond if someone offered to literally wash your feet?

How has your definition of "service" changed this week?

DAY 6

Be joyful always; pray continually; give thanks in all circumstances, for this is God's will for you in Christ Jesus.

1 Thessalonians 5:16–18

God "will give to each person according to what he has done." To those who by persistence in doing good seek glory, honor and immortality, he will give eternal life. But for those who are self-seeking and who reject the truth and follow evil, there will be wrath and anger.

Romans 2:6–8

Nobody should seek his own good, but the good of others.

1 Corinthians 10:24

Watching Val in public is like watching an ongoing train wreck. Every time you're out to eat with her, she's incredibly rude. Waiters never move fast enough. Food is never right. She's beyond rude. Unfortunately, Val's rudeness doesn't end there.

People never drive fast enough, rooms are never organized right, movies are lame, TV is boring, friends are stupid. And, on really bad days, you're an idiot. She never says anything positive or lifts a hand to help. You often wonder why you hang out with her.

The fact that Val goes to church is laughable. She's just not the kind of person who "belongs" in church—with the kind of attitude she has.

Everything that comes out of her mouth is negative, condescending, and downright mean.

Val goes to youth group too, which is also like watching a train wreck. Most people would try to put their best foot forward there, at least try to blend in. Valerie doesn't seem to care about putting her best foot forward. She is her normal complaining and rude self at church, where she leaves a path of bruised and damaged feelings in her wake. People wonder what hit them after she passes by.

The kid who dislikes everyone.

The kid who's always watching out for herself.

The kid who never serves.

↑ Looking Up

How would it feel to be Val's friend? How about her enemy?

What kind of advice would you give her?

How would serving others impact Val's worldview?

DAY 7

But be sure to fear the LORD and serve him faithfully with all your heart; consider what great things he has done for you.

1 Samuel 12:24

I thank Christ Jesus our Lord, who has given me strength, that he considered me faithful, appointing me to his service.

1 Timothy 1:12

And he said: "I tell you the truth, unless you change and become like little children, you will never enter the kingdom of heaven."

Matthew 18:3

Serving others isn't easy; it can be messy, annoying, dirty, tiring, and frustrating, among other things. (Just ask your parents, the janitor at your school, or your pastor, if you don't believe me.)

So why do it?

Because when we're serving others out of obedience to God, the blessings far outweigh the frustrations. The thing is, God doesn't *need* our help; rather, he allows our help so we can experience the joy of serving.

Want a good visual example of how God sees you and me? Try this activity:

Recruit a young child (brother, neighbor, friend, etc.) to help you with one of your chores (making cookies would even be better). Be sure to explain it as a team project, something you two will be working on together.

Let the child helper do as many of the steps as possible, as long as it's not dangerous. Be encouraging and patient. More than likely, your task will take much longer with the extra "help." And there's probably more mess than usual.

But when the task is done, take a good look at the child's face—your partner, assistant, and helper. If he or she is like most elementary school children, the joys of helping you far outweigh any mess, annoyance, or frustration.

When God allows us to help him by serving others, he's allowing us to work alongside him, to partner with him. When we offer ourselves willingly, knowing he's right beside us, he will bless us beyond comprehension.

When you serve, you are a tool in God's hands. He chooses each of us to do amazing things, to do big things as well as small things. Our part is our willingness. The more willing we are to be used, the more often God will recruit us for his glory.

What have you learned about serving from this activity?

Using what you've learned from this illustration, how would you explain the importance of serving others to your best friend?

How can you apply what you've learned and the truth you've discovered from Scripture about this topic?

WHY SHOULD I CARRY MY CROSS?

DAY 1

Anyone who does not take his cross and follow me is not worthy of me. Whoever finds his life will lose it, and whoever loses his life for my sake will find it.

Matthew 10:38–39

For we know that our old self was crucified with him so that the body of sin might be done away with, that we should no longer be slaves to sin—because anyone who has died has been freed from sin.

Romans 6:6–7

I have been crucified with Christ and I no longer live, but Christ lives in me. The life I live in the body, I live by faith in the Son of God, who loved me and gave himself for me.

Galatians 2:20

You can volunteer for all kinds of things. Imagine you have three months free, without any obligations. You don't have to work; you don't have school. Try to think of some ways you could spend your time . . .

Here are some common summer volunteer positions:

Serving dinner at a soup kitchen

Spending time at a homeless shelter

Working with inner-city kids

Helping at a kids' camp

What are some things you have done or would like to do as a volunteer?

- _____
- _____
- _____
- _____

Volunteer work always requires a measure of selfless giving; if you choose to spend time at the local nursing home once a week, it definitely cuts other activities out of your schedule.

If you've ever willingly sacrificed your time for others, though, you know the rewards involved are truly immeasurable. And some volunteer work can even be fun: coaching at a youth basketball camp, delivering Christmas gifts to needy families, teaching a child to read.

My sister just returned from Mexico where she and her husband and a motley crew from their church helped build two houses for indigent single-parent families. It was a costly, time-consuming trip that provided little in the way of luxury for any of the volunteers. My sister had to find child care for their three young children while they were gone, and they worked hard every day, all day to get the buildings completed on time.

And yet she and her husband had more fun on that trip than on one they took a year ago to attend baseball spring training in Arizona. Why? Because they saw a need and were able to fill it. Because they willingly gave of themselves. Because, for an entire week, they took up their cross and died to self.

This week we'll learn how important it is to carry our cross, and we'll talk about some real ways we can do that. Carrying our cross requires sacrifice. It requires effort. It requires taking a closer look at the one who first carried his cross—Jesus.

↑ Looking Up

What do you think it means to "die to self"?

Why is it so hard for us to die to self?

Who are some famous people you know who have made a commitment to die to self?

DAY 2

Then Jesus said to his disciples, "If anyone would come after me, he must deny himself and take up his cross and follow me. For whoever wants to save his life will lose it, but whoever loses his life for me will find it."

Matthew 16:24–25

And anyone who does not carry his cross and follow me cannot be my disciple.

Luke 14:27

I will give you a new heart and put a new spirit in you; I will remove from you your heart of stone and give you a heart of flesh.

Ezekiel 36:26

My kids collect toothbrushes. I know, it's kind of disgusting. Well, they don't actually have a collection of old toothbrushes, they just really hate throwing away a used (but beloved) toothbrush in place of a shiny, straight, bristly, plaque-free new one. It's gotten so ridiculous that we have a toothbrush rule in our home: no new toothbrushes until the old ones have been chucked for good. Forever. Never to be seen again, and I mean it.

I used to pretend not to notice when they kept their toothbrushes long past any usefulness. I'd hand them a new one, knowing it would share the tray in the drawer with last year's model. Then I learned a thing or two while waiting my turn in the dentist's chair. Apparently (OK, don't get grossed out on me) old toothbrushes can be the residence of a variety of harmful bacteria that can cause infections.

Buying a new toothbrush and innocently storing it with the old is sort of like a healthy person snuggling up with a coughing, hacking, sneezing, contagious person and expecting to stay healthy. Yick. Kinda makes you shudder a little, huh?

Well, guess what? Our old nature, our sin nature, is simply loaded with harmful spiritual bacteria. Contagious, harmful bacteria. Don't even think about getting a flu shot and committing to extra hand washing. Spiritual bacteria is impervious to your measly efforts at defense.

The only solution is to throw out, put off, and bury your old sin nature. It's only when the old is completely gone that Jesus can put a new heart inside of you, one that his Holy Spirit lives inside.

OK, let's get specific. What does it mean to bury your old sin nature?

It means asking forgiveness from God.

It means genuinely asking God to change you from the inside out.

It means making some changes in your life so you are not tempted with the same old sins.

It means making a conscious decision to daily set aside that old grungy toothbrush—er, sin nature.

This is not a one-time deal. Salvation is a one-time deal; once you're saved, you're saved for eternity. However, your old sin nature, until you get to heaven, will try to sneak back in the drawer with your new self and try to rub off on it. Don't let it!

If you are tempted to steal, shop with a friend.

If you are tempted to cheat at school, sit near the teacher's desk.

If you are tempted to skip your daily devotions, ask someone to hold you accountable.

If you're tempted by sexual images, protect what you allow your eyes to see.

The war against spiritual plaque is a daily one. Jesus longs to see his Spirit working in and through you. He asks that you deny yourself, pick up your cross, and follow him. Failing to take measures to protect yourself against spiritual decay is like never throwing an old toothbrush away. And don't even get me started on flossing . . .

↑ Looking Up

What are some areas of your old sin nature you need to bury?

What are some things you can do to protect yourself from temptation?

Who is someone you trust who could hold you accountable, to help you remember to be diligent in daily dying to self?

DAY 3

O LORD, I call to you; come quickly to me. Hear my voice when I call to you. May my prayer be set before you like incense; may the lifting up of my hands be like the evening sacrifice.

Psalm 141:1–2

My guilt has overwhelmed me like a burden too heavy to bear.

Psalm 38:4

Those controlled by the sinful nature cannot please God. You, however, are controlled not by the sinful nature but by the Spirit, if the Spirit of God lives in you. And if anyone does not have the Spirit of Christ, he does not belong to Christ.

Romans 8:8–9

I cheated on a test once. It was in Mr. Hetland's first-period seventh-grade geography class. I couldn't remember the name of some obscure mountain range in Africa. I hadn't meant to cheat, but as my neighbor walked by with her test, I couldn't help but see the answer—Tibesti Mountains, located in the Sahara Desert of Northern Africa.

Checking to see if anyone had seen my glance, I quickly filled in the answer on my test. Then I turned my paper in. Then my stomach started to hurt. Then my head started to hurt. Then my pulse became erratic. Then I realized the whole "cheating on your geography test" thing wasn't all it was cracked up to be.

Because I really respected Mr. Hetland, I had to come clean. As embarrassing as it was to admit to cheating, I fumbled through my explanation and left room 210 with a clean conscience and an eraser smudge in the space previously occupied by "Tibesti Mountain Range."

I've never forgotten how it felt to lie to someone I admired. And I knew in my heart that God had seen my actions and was disappointed with my choice. You can bet I never again cheated on a school test.

I wonder sometimes how I would have felt had I not admitted the truth. I knew I had let my teacher, God, and myself down. Thankfully, God prompted me to listen and to obey him, to admit my sin and accept forgiveness, and move on. I know, I know—it was *only* a seventh-grade geography test. It was also a test of my character, and only by the prompting of the Holy Spirit did I pass.

Too many people ignore the prompting of the Holy Spirit. Too many people are carrying around the burden of sin and guilt. Dying to self and the old sin nature releases the burden of guilt. It allows you to let go of all the times you've let someone you love down, all the times you've let yourself down, all the times you've let God down.

It's only when we die to our old sin nature that we are free to love, serve, obey, and worship God with a clean conscience. Yes, there may be a few eraser smudges on your moral résumé, but the forgiveness of God totally erases all of that. His mercy is kind of like supernatural white-out—it covers even the toughest "mistakes."

Listen to the Holy Spirit's nudge toward repentance. Allow him to remove that heavy burden you've been carting around all by yourself. It may be a little embarrassing at first to come clean with the Savior, but you'll feel much better in the end.

↑ Looking Up

Can you think of any "character tests" you've encountered? How did you do?

Do you have a particular burden of past sins you'd like to lay at God's feet?

Although God is not pleased when we sin, how do you think it makes him feel when we repent?

DAY 4

Set your minds on things above, not on earthly things. For you died, and your life is now hidden with Christ in God. When Christ, who is your life, appears, then you also will appear with him in glory.

Colossians 3:2–4

Here is a trustworthy saying: If we died with him, we will also live with him.

2 Timothy 2:11

Jesus said to her, "I am the resurrection and the life. He who believes in me will live, even though he dies; and whoever lives and believes in me will never die. Do you believe this?"

John 11:25–26

Heard any good news/bad news jokes lately? Here's a classic:

Doctor: I have some good news and I have some bad news.

Patient: What's the good news?

Doctor: The good news is that the tests you took showed that you have 24 hours to live.

Patient: What? That's the good news? What's the bad news?

Doctor: The bad news is that I forgot to call you yesterday!

I know—*groan, sigh, argh*—very lame. You get a lot of good news/bad news skits at junior high and high school camps. And trust me, I went to a lot of junior high and high school camps.

So all this week we've been learning about carrying our cross, discovering that Jesus requires us to die to self before we can truly become a follower of his. To the outside world, this is the bad news. Dying to self requires sacrifice, hardship, vulnerability, and surrendering yourself to God. Anyone who has experienced dying to self and has seen the benefits of drawing closer to the Savior knows it's really not bad news—it's just hard news.

But what's the good news? Once we've died to self, we are promised life with Jesus in heaven for eternity. In case you missed that all-important word, *eternity*, let me define it for you:

eternity • noun (pl. **eternities**) 1 infinite or unending time.

Infinite and unending. Kind of hard to wrap your mind around the concept, isn't it?

The first four books of the New Testament—Matthew, Mark, Luke, and John—are also referred to as the Gospels. It's no coincidence that the word *gospel* means "good news" in Greek.

Jesus's life and ministry, as recorded in the Gospels, is the essence of all good news. He came to die so that we may live. We didn't deserve it. We didn't earn it. It's pretty amazingly cool, excellent, tremendous, awesome good news. In fact, it just doesn't get any better than that.

↑ Looking Up

How do you feel when you get to give someone really good news?
How do you feel when you hear really good news?
Have you shared the Good News, the gospel, with anyone before?

DAY 5

Praise be to the Lord, to God our Savior, who daily bears our burdens.

Psalm 68:19

Surely he took up our infirmities and carried our sorrows, yet we considered him stricken by God, smitten by him, and afflicted.

Isaiah 53:4

He tends his flock like a shepherd: He gathers the lambs in his arms and carries them close to his heart; he gently leads those that have young.

Isaiah 40:11

Pulling yourself up by your own bootstraps. Ever heard that expression?

It is believed to have originated several hundred years ago. Riding boots were fashioned with a strap at the back to pull them on. Since the boots were made out of fairly thick and stiff material, pulling up one's boots was no easy task.

The act of "pulling yourself up by your own bootstraps" would mean using your own efforts to raise yourself up off the ground. Although many of us don't have bootstraps (unless you're into horses and 4-H), we get the gist of this well-used phrase. I researched a bit online and found some good translations:

To leverage yourself to success from a small beginning

To have self-empowerment in the face of adversity

To raise yourself in the world exclusively through your own
    efforts

I've got one word for you: hogwash.

We've already learned that anything we do is only accomplished by the power of God and his strength. To try to raise yourself in the world *exclusively* through your own efforts would be foolhardy at best, and ineffective to be sure. Have you ever seen anyone raise himself off the ground by pulling up his boots? OK, other than professional illusionists, it ain't gonna happen, my friend.

What does the Bible say about all this? What does carrying one's cross have to do with this? I found a good Scripture to get us started. It's found in Exodus 3, right after Moses sees the angel of the LORD in flames of fire from within a bush.

"God called to [Moses] from within the bush, . . . 'Do not come any closer. . . . Take off your sandals, for the place where you are standing is holy ground'" (Exodus 3:4–5).

Back away from the bush, Moses. This place is too hot, too holy, too much for you to handle. God didn't want Moses any closer, not because he was invading on God's turf. Not because he wanted to put Moses in his place. Not because he was angry with Moses.

God told Moses to take off his sandals to acknowledge God's sovereignty and holiness. To show Moses that God alone could handle the fire. That burning bush became symbolic of the things in Moses's life that were too much of a burden for him to shoulder on his own: confronting his people after he had abandoned them, confronting Pharaoh for the freedom of the Hebrews, crossing the Red Sea, leading the Israelites to the Promised Land, defeating their enemies in battle.

God showed Moses that the only way to survive and succeed was to get rid of his bootstraps and rely on God. Why? Because God planned to carry Moses through all of this. God alone was strong enough to handle the heat of adversity.

When we die to self, we die to our own efforts. We die to the impulse to do everything by ourselves. To raise ourselves in the world exclusively by our own efforts.

Back away from the fire. It's too hot—you'll only get burned. Take off your bootstraps and honor the one who longs to carry you through every difficulty you will face in your life.

↑ Looking Up

What are some difficulties you have gone through?

In what ways have you tried to pull yourself up by your own bootstraps?

What aspects of God's character have you learned about and grown to love this week?

DAY 6

In all their distress he too was distressed, and the angel of his presence saved them. In his love and mercy he redeemed them; he lifted them up and carried them all the days of old.

Isaiah 63:9

It is for freedom that Christ has set us free. Stand firm, then, and do not let yourselves be burdened again by a yoke of slavery.

Galatians 5:1

And this is the testimony: God has given us eternal life, and this life is in his Son. He who has the Son has life; he who does not have the Son of God does not have life.

1 John 5:11–12

Maybe you know someone like Rich. He's the guy who stays after youth group to put away the chairs. He's the guy who rakes his yard, the neighbor's yard, and he'd probably rake your yard if you let him. He's the first to show up at a volunteer event and the last to leave. His life seems to be spent going from one act of service to another.

Rich seems to serve because he *needs* to serve.

It all becomes clear the first time you invite him over.

The two of you were hanging out at lunch, and you ask if he wants to come over after school. Vegging out with a video game sounds like a great idea, so you challenge him to a PlayStation 2 game.

Rich arrives, but before you get started, he asks if you need help with any chores. Wow, not many of your friends make that offer! But no, you tell him, you've already done them.

You beat Rich three times in a row. He's good, but each time he gets close to winning, you get the feeling that he's backing off. It doesn't seem to bother Rich when he loses. He actually loses at a lot of games, and not just video games.

Rich has just agreed to your challenge of one final round, when your mom comes home.

Before you can say hello, Rich jumps to his feet and runs over to your mom. "Can I take those bags for you? Do you have any more groceries in the car?"

You and Rich bring in the rest of the groceries. As you set down the last bag, you look up to see Rich hurrying toward your mom again. She's carrying a load of laundry.

"Here, let me take that. Where would you like it?" he says, reaching for the basket.

Your mom gives Rich a funny look. "No, thanks, I'm fine."

You suggest to Rich that you play that last game. As you get ready to start, Rich says something strange.

"I hope your mom likes me."

You look at him. "Why wouldn't she?"

"Well, I didn't help much. My parents say I don't think about other people enough." He shakes his head. "No matter how hard I try to help, I can't ever seem to please people."

↑ Looking Up

What problem do you see with Rich's motivation to serve others?

Who is he trying to please—other people or God?

What advice would you give Rich about learning to be selfless?

DAY 7

He answered: "'Love the Lord your God with all your heart and with all your soul and with all your strength and with all your mind'; and, 'Love your neighbor as yourself.'"

Luke 10:27

My command is this: Love each other as I have loved you. Greater love has no
one than this, that he lay down his life for his friends.

John 15:12–13

For the message of the cross is foolishness to those who are perishing, but to us
who are being saved it is the power of God.

1 Corinthians 1:18

You know, after a while, talking about carrying your cross begins to
sound like one long sound bite. We know we need to do it; we read
about how we're supposed to do it; and we hear from spiritual leaders
the struggles we'll face when we do it. Before too long, the idea of actually carrying our cross is reduced to an idea or a concept too difficult
to attain. Many of us may get to the point where we ask ourselves,
"Why even bother?"

But why, exactly, is self-sacrifice so tough? Why can't we just decide
to surrender ourselves and carry our crosses? What is the big deal?

To answer that question, try the following activity. Ask a friend to
sit with you and have a conversation. To get the best results, you may
want to record your session. In the period of about ten minutes, count
how many times you say the words "me," "mine," "I," and "my."

What you're bound to discover is that it's nearly impossible to hold
a conversation without using those particular personal pronouns. We
talk about ourselves almost as much as we think about ourselves. That
fact doesn't make us bad people; it just makes us . . . people.

The big deal about carrying our cross is the simple fact that human
beings from the outset of creation have struggled with placing too much
priority on self. And you're not any different.

When you break it down, the core of all sin is selfishness. It's the
root of all evil. By agreeing to carry our cross, by striving to put others
before us, we recognize our inherent selfishness and the need to do
something about it.

And it's not easy. But in order to be a growing disciple of Jesus
Christ, it's imperative that you follow him on the road of self-sacrifice.
If you attempt such a feat on your own, you'll fail, plain and simple.

But when you stop looking at your own efforts and accept God's help, you'll experience the supernatural, saving power of the cross.

↑ Looking Up

What have you learned about carrying your cross from this activity?

Using what you've learned from this illustration, how would you explain the overemphasis of self in our culture?

How can you apply what you've learned and the truth you've discovered from Scripture about this topic?

WHY SHOULD I BE
DISCIPLED?

DAY 1

The fear of the LORD is the beginning of knowledge, but fools despise wisdom and discipline.

Proverbs 1:7

And we pray this in order that you may live a life worthy of the Lord and may please him in every way: bearing fruit in every good work, growing in the knowledge of God.

Colossians 1:10

We ought always to thank God for you, brothers, and rightly so, because your faith is growing more and more, and the love every one of you has for each other is increasing.

2 Thessalonians 1:3

Put yourself in the place of a pipe cleaner for a sec.

You remember what a pipe cleaner is, don't you? It's that bendy wire thing covered with furry craft stuff. You probably used it a lot in elementary school.

OK, you're a fuzzy, bendy pipe cleaner. Think about what life would be like (supposing pipe cleaners are capable of rational thought). The pipe cleaner is completely under the control of the person molding it. It has little input into what it's shaped into or how it's formed. The pipe cleaner doesn't resist much. It can't.

Being discipled is a lot like being a pipe cleaner. When you're being discipled, you're allowing yourself to be molded and shaped at the hands of someone else.

Let's talk about what being discipled is *not* about: it doesn't mean that you allow a mentor to teach you untruth, and it doesn't mean that you allow them to mold you into something God doesn't intend for you.

With that in mind, the one who disciples you must be someone you admire, someone you trust, someone who cares about you. Most important, your mentor must have evidence of a living, solid, growing, mature faith in Jesus Christ.

List three people who you think would be good mentors for you:

- _____
- _____
- _____

This week we're talking about discipleship and your growth. Spiritual growth is important for several reasons:

1. Jesus instructs us to learn from others.
2. The Bible provides examples of individuals who learned from others.
3. If you're not growing, you're molding.
4. As you grow, so does your love for God and for one another.

One of the best ways you can grow is through being discipled.

↑ Looking Up

Can you think of some biblical characters who needed to be discipled?

Why are some people content to stay in one spot spiritually rather than grow?

On a scale of 1–10 (10 being a spiritual genius), how would you rate your knowledge of God? What would you like that number to be?

DAY 2

Therefore go and make disciples of all nations, baptizing them in the name of the Father and of the Son and of the Holy Spirit, and teaching them to obey everything I have commanded you. And surely I am with you always, to the very end of the age.

Matthew 28:19–20

This is to my Father's glory, that you bear much fruit, showing yourselves to be my disciples.

John 15:8

Jesus went up on a mountainside and called to him those he wanted, and they came to him. He appointed twelve—designating them apostles—that they might be with him and that he might send them out to preach and to have authority to drive out demons.

Mark 3:13–15

If you were the Son of God coming down to live among sinful man, who would you choose as friends? As disciples? As students? As the ones who would be sent out to the world to proclaim the good news of salvation? Remember, you're restricted to twelve. Here's some of my top picks (oh, and we're not limited to time constraints here): C. S. Lewis, Oswald Chambers, Dietrich Bonhoeffer, Billy Graham, James Dobson, Chuck Colson, Charles Swindoll, D. L. Moody, and A. W. Tozer.

What great men of God! What amazing things we could accomplish together! I would choose individuals worthy of respect, of intellectual recognition, of power, fame, prestige, and influence.

That's why I'm not Jesus.

Although I profoundly respect the men listed above, they were not at all the type Jesus chose. He looked at the heart of the men he chose and knew he could transfigure them from the inside out. And none of them could take the credit, because they were sinful, unassuming men before they encountered their Savior. Jesus picked a motley crew, to be sure. Here's a list of them:

Peter & Andrew—a hotheaded fisherman and his brother
James & John—brothers whom Jesus named "Sons of Thunder" because of their tendency to rush to judgment; also fishermen

Philip—a fisherman too often concerned with the finances of the group

Bartholomew—aka Nathanael

Thomas—aka Doubting Thomas

Matthew—a former tax collector, one who was hated by the Jews

James—a possible brother to Matthew

Thaddaeus—aka Judas (not the betrayer)

Simon—the zealot, a fanatical nationalist of Judea

Judas—the one who betrayed Jesus

Although their résumés before Jesus aren't too impressive, their sacrifices for the cause of Christ are downright amazing. Many of them were killed for their beliefs, and all of them suffered.

Jesus chose these men three years prior to his crucifixion. He used that time to teach, train, shepherd, and disciple them for the task he would give them. He set an excellent example for the rest of us to follow. What an amazing thing that he has called you and me to his kingdom work. Our spiritual résumés are probably not as impressive as we'd like them to be. Don't worry, though. Jesus is able to transform us from the inside out, just as he did for hotheaded Peter.

↑ Looking Up

Can you name the twelve disciples?

Which one do you relate to the most?

Using your knowledge of the Old Testament, why do you think Jesus chose *twelve* men to be his disciples? Why not eleven? Why not thirteen?

DAY 3

Hold on to instruction, do not let it go; guard it well, for it is your life.

Proverbs 4:13

Listen to advice and accept instruction, and in the end you will be wise.

Proverbs 19:20

Apply your heart to instruction and your ears to words of knowledge.

Proverbs 23:12

In case you haven't noticed, the book of Proverbs, written by King Solomon, is the Wisdom book. There are a lot of verses pertaining to instruction, learning, teaching, knowledge, the foolish, and the wise. In fact, in a mere thirty-one chapters, the word *fool* is used thirty-seven times. Apparently, King Solomon knew people pretty well.

How would you define a fool?

_____

_____

_____

_____

Here's what the Bible has to say:

The fool says in his heart, "There is no God." (Psalm 14:1)

A fool spurns his father's discipline. (Proverbs 15:5)

The way of a fool seems right to him. (Proverbs 12:15)

A fool finds no pleasure in understanding. (Proverbs 18:2)

Every fool is quick to quarrel. (Proverbs 20:3)

As a dog returns to its vomit, so a fool repeats his folly. (Proverbs 26:11)

He who trusts in himself is a fool. (Proverbs 28:26)

Well, those verses are pretty disturbing (especially the one about the dog and the vomit). The counterpart to these verses repeats the theme of learning from others, searching out wisdom, listening to your elders, and so on. The book of Proverbs is essentially a commercial for discipleship!

Reading. Listening. Learning. Are you catching on? Discipleship under the care and guidance of someone wise and understanding of the Word of God is your ticket from foolish (remember the vomit thing?) to wise. The wise are those who acknowledge and love God; the wise are those who trust God; the wise are those who seek God.

A fool is someone . . . else.

↑ Looking Up

How does the world view individuals who trust in themselves?

What kind of people does society see as wise?

Do you have to know everything there is to know in order to be wise?

DAY 4

When a wise man is instructed, he gets knowledge.

Proverbs 21:11

Instruct a wise man and he will be wiser still; teach a righteous man and he will add to his learning.

Proverbs 9:9

But grow in the grace and knowledge of our Lord and Savior Jesus Christ. To him be glory both now and forever! Amen.

2 Peter 3:18

I live in the Northwest. We get a lot of rain there. A lot of rain. It is rarely completely dry, even in the summer months. Because of all the moisture, we northwesterners have quite a time keeping up with the problem of . . . *mold.* I've lost more than one leather item of value because of that green fuzzy stuff.

The mold problem is not going to be resolved anytime soon. Those of us resigned to live in a lush but moldy green region have learned some basics about mold prevention.

1. Locate and fix all leaks.
2. Raise the temperature of the room.
3. Pay attention to stagnant water.

Mold loves to grow in moist areas where water has been left unattended. It thrives in tepid environments, which are neither hot nor cold, the same preferred by bacteria and other microorganisms.

Kind of reminds me of spiritual sluggishness. In the Bible, a thriving faith evidenced by the indwelling of the Holy Spirit is likened to flowing water. Jesus said in John 7:38, "Whoever believes in me, as the Scripture has said, streams of living water will flow from within him."

Living water is active; it is cool, fresh, and satisfying. Dead water harbors bacteria; it is filled with mud and contaminants. Living water represents active and dynamic growth; dead water symbolizes apathy, laziness, and lethargy.

To sum it up: If you're not growing for God, you're molding in mediocrity.

Unfortunately, the spiritual mold problem isn't going away anytime soon either. Here are some steps to take for spiritual mold prevention:

1. Locate and fix all leaks—Are you doing so many other things that you don't have time to spend with God? Eliminate some of the leaks and make time for him.
2. Raise the temperature—Crank up the heat! Get involved with a Bible study whose members are on fire for Jesus. Pray for God to light a fire in you as well.

3. Pay attention to stagnant water—Find someone you trust and respect to help mentor you, to hold you accountable, and to push you toward growth; this person operates as your mold monitor.

OK, you've got the tools. Don't settle for moldy mediocrity—get growing for God!

↑Looking Up

When was the last time you studied the Scriptures?
Why is it easier for us to grow apathetic when no one is watching?
Do you have any leaks that need immediate attention?

DAY 5

But solid food is for the mature, who by constant use have trained themselves to distinguish good from evil. Therefore let us leave the elementary teachings about Christ and go on to maturity.

Hebrews 5:14–6:1

Like newborn babies, crave pure spiritual milk, so that by it you may grow up in your salvation, now that you have tasted that the Lord is good.

1 Peter 2:2–3

Taste and see that the LORD is good; blessed is the man who takes refuge in him.

Psalm 34:8

Got milk?

I remember babysitting for my three-week-old cousin many years ago. I was thirteen and, to be honest, a little out of my comfort zone. Tiny babies are fragile, wrinkly, floppy, and very LOUD. Especially when they're hungry.

My aunt and uncle needed a break from parenthood and decided to leave their only child in the care of an insecure, bewildered, and frightened teenager—me! As they walked out the door, I don't know who looked more alarmed—the baby, my aunt, or me. I was equipped with diapers (cloth—ugh!), spit-up rags (double ugh!), the restaurant phone number, and a bottle.

Unfortunately, my cousin had never tried a bottle before; although he couldn't yet talk, he communicated quite clearly how he felt about having a substitute for his mother. I had no idea how hard an infant could scream. Or how long. By the time his parents came through the door, he and I were snuggled down in the rocking chair bawling our eyes out.

Being discipled by a mature Christian is important in your pursuit of spiritual milk (aka biblical truths and principles). First Peter compares the hearty wails of an infant to a believer bent on getting more of God. And just like my cousin couldn't settle for second best, we as Christians need to hold out for righteous teachings from the Holy Scriptures.

Some of you may be thinking, "How in the world could I be satisfied with only milk?" Well, that's because you're forgetting all the delectable dairy goods derived from milk. Try to see the different chapters in the Bible as varied milk products.

2% Milk—The Law (Genesis, Exodus, Leviticus, Numbers, Deuteronomy)

Cottage Cheese—The History of Israel (Joshua through Esther)

Butter—The Poetry Books (Job through Song of Songs)

Cheese—The Prophets (Isaiah through Malachi)

Eggnog—The Gospels (Matthew, Mark, Luke, John)

Cream—History/Letters (Acts through Jude)

Ice Cream—Prophecy (Revelation)

There now, makes you kinda hungry just reading about them, doesn't it? If you're a believer in Jesus Christ, you have the Spirit of God living inside of you. His Spirit can thrive only with the nutrients from Bible study and prayer. You may have some friends who are spiritually lactose intolerant (nonbelievers). Pray for them that, by watching you, God will whet their appetite for him.

Are you hungry and thirsty for the Word of God in your life?
What book of the Bible are you interested in studying?
In what ways do we sometimes settle for second best?

DAY 6

[Jesus] replied, "Every plant that my heavenly Father has not planted will be pulled up by the roots. Leave them; they are blind guides. If a blind man leads a blind man, both will fall into a pit."

Matthew 15:13–14

He who heeds discipline shows the way to life, but whoever ignores correction leads others astray.

Proverbs 10:17

Cursed is the man who leads the blind astray on the road.

Deuteronomy 27:18

Adam's dad has been an adult volunteer in your youth group since you started attending church. He's considered the cool dad. He takes the family skiing every Christmas break, and he drives a very cool car. Everyone likes Adam's dad because he's cool, but he also seems to care about the kids too.

You know Adam's dad real well. You've spent the night with Adam loads of times, and you've seen a completely different side of his dad. He's always angry at Adam for something. Actually, he's always angry at everyone in the family. Adam's dad yells. And, on the nights you've slept over, when his dad wasn't yelling, he was strange. Strange beyond normal parental strangeness. The one time you remember most is the time he and Adam's mom went out for dinner. When they came home, Adam's dad was obviously drunk. He kept trying to hug everyone.

After youth group one evening last week, Adam's dad approached you. The youth pastor has been encouraging the adults to take on a student and disciple them. Adam's dad wants to disciple you. He wants to meet with you once a week and talk about God.

You know too much about Adam's dad to take him seriously. The things you've observed about him make you uncomfortable; in fact there's not much about Adam's dad you respect at all. What should you do?

↑ Looking Up

What kind of a person do you need to be in order to disciple someone?

What are some things you would want to tell the youth pastor?

What are some things you would want to tell Adam and his dad?

DAY 7

Does not the potter have the right to make out of the same lump of clay some pottery for noble purposes and some for common use?

Romans 9:21

Since my youth, O God, you have taught me, and to this day I declare your marvelous deeds.

Psalm 71:17

> Let the word of Christ dwell in you richly as you teach and admonish one another with all wisdom, and as you sing psalms, hymns and spiritual songs with gratitude in your hearts to God.
>
> Colossians 3:16

Discipleship is a huge, often nebulous word. We toss around the idea of discipleship or of being discipled all the time. What's so important about being discipled? Why should you allow someone to influence you? To learn more about being discipled, get a piece of string, some paper, and a pencil and do the following:

> On top of a blank piece of paper, form the string into the shape of a human being. Now carefully trace around it with a pencil.
>
> On another sheet of paper, lay out the string in the shape of a four-legged animal (like a dog or cat). Trace around it.
>
> On a third piece of paper, form the string into the shape of a square. Again, trace around it.

Now that you've done all of that, pick up the string and lay it out straight in front of you. Spread out your three drawings. When you look at the drawings, remember this—one string made all three shapes. Who made the shapes? You did, using the string.

Now, think about discipleship. You (the string), in the hands of an older, wiser, godly person, can be fashioned into any shape. With someone's influence, you can be formed into an amazing man or woman of God. You can be formed into a world changer. You can also be formed into a plain, ordinary, boring person who never grows, never stretches, never accepts challenges, and never reaches to change or shape someone else.

Imagine yourself as a piece of string. Imagine that those you allow to influence you really do shape you into a variety of things. It's your job to choose the life shapers. It's your job to choose the right people who can, by God's direction, form and disciple you into a God-honoring shape.

You have to find a person you trust, look up to, and admire who will be willing to form you. Look for a godly, prayerful person who is both willing to tell you the truth and willing to put in the time that discipleship takes. Don't be afraid to ask your parents or youth pastor for their input. Pray about your decision and ask God for wisdom. Look for confirmation that your choice is a good one. Here are three helpful steps to check the confirmation process:

1. Does your choice go against or with God's Word?
2. Do the spiritually mature adults in your life agree with your decision?
3. Do you have God's peace about your decision?

↑ Looking Up

What have you learned about being discipled from this activity?

Using what you've learned from this illustration, how would you explain the importance of being discipled to your best friend?

How can you apply what you've learned and the truth you've discovered from Scripture about this topic?

WHY DO I NEED THE HOLY SPIRIT?

DAY 1

In the beginning God created the heavens and the earth. Now the earth was formless and empty, darkness was over the surface of the deep, and the Spirit of God was hovering over the waters.

Genesis 1:1–2

Can you fathom the mysteries of God? Can you probe the limits of the Almighty?

Job 11:7

However, as it is written: "No eye has seen, no ear has heard, no mind has conceived what God has prepared for those who love him"—but God has revealed it to us by his Spirit. The Spirit searches all things, even the deep things of God.

1 Corinthians 2:9–10

A group of people standing in a worship service mumbling in a strange language, their arms raised and swaying back and forth.

A man preaching in your city park, his face red with frenzied anger. Spit forms in the corners of his mouth. He doesn't look at you as you pass. Doesn't even get distracted when another passerby throws a hamburger wrapper at him.

A lady in your church during a worship service. She's giving a testimony about how the Holy Spirit healed her of some serious disease.

A television evangelist praying in the Spirit for you to send more money for his ministry. Praying that God's Spirit would make you feel guilty for denying his request.

A friend you admire and respect who joyfully explains how he was led by the Spirit to go on a mission trip to Mexico and how that trip has changed his life.

Who in the world is the Holy Spirit? What does he do? Is the Holy Spirit a "he"? How do we know?

People have all kinds of beliefs about the Holy Spirit. Some believe that he's a doctor and heals us of every awful sickness. Others believe that the Holy Spirit hits you like a boulder falling from a cliff fifty feet above you.

Below, write three things you know for sure about the Holy Spirit.

- _____

- _____

- _____

This week we're tackling the Holy Spirit. We'll discover who he is, what he does, and how he affects our lives. Most of all, you'll get in touch with this gift of God's Helper, given to us to make us more like Christ.

↑ Looking Up

Have you ever tried to explain the Holy Spirit to someone? Why is it so difficult?

Can you think of a situation when you encountered God's Spirit?

What are some questions you have about the Holy Spirit?

DAY 2

For you did not receive a spirit that makes you a slave again to fear, but you received the Spirit of sonship. And by him we cry, "Abba, Father." The Spirit himself testifies with our spirit that we are God's children.

Romans 8:15–16

And I will ask the Father, and he will give you another Counselor to be with your forever—the Spirit of truth. The world cannot accept him, because it nei-

ther sees him nor knows him. But you know him, for he lives with you and will
be in you.

John 14:16–17

But I tell you the truth: It is for your good that I am going away. Unless I go
away, the Counselor will not come to you; but if I go, I will send him to you.

John 16:7

I want you to notice the word "he" in the above verses. In fact, count
how many "he/hims" refer to the Holy Spirit. I got eight. Eight references in five verses that show the Spirit to be a person, not an "it."
The words spoken in the verses from John were those of Jesus Christ,
the resident authority of all things of God. His word on the subject is
final. Period.

OK, moving on. A *spirit* can be defined as the disposition that fills
and directs the soul of a person. Let's follow this through sort of like
a mathematical equation.

If:

1. the Spirit of God is a HE . . .
2. a spirit is defined as the being that affects and governs everything
   about us . . .
3. as believers we are filled with God's Spirit . . .

Then (this is just so cool):

1. We are filled, affected, governed, and influenced by the very
   person of God. When we ask Jesus into our lives and accept his
   sacrifice for our sins, God infuses everything about himself into
   our sinful, lost, fragile persons forever. You can't force him out,
   push him out, or lose him. He's a permanent fixture in the living
   room of our hearts.

The importance of this truth is the fact that many people do not recognize its importance! (You may want to reread that last sentence—it's
confusing, but true.)

So many Christians are walking around unaware that the Creator of the universe resides inside of them, myself included. We pray things like,

"God, be with me!"
"God, be near me!"
"God, where are you?"

These cries are similar to those uttered by King David all through the Psalms. They are legitimate pleas for God to draw near and wrap his presence around us in the midst of pain, confusion, and fear.

And it's OK to pray these prayers. But realize the following truth: He is near us. He has not left us. Jesus's use of the personal pronoun, *he*, in today's verses reveals to us that God is with us. You can't get any closer than being *within* someone!

I've always wondered what it was like for Jesus's disciples to physically touch, see, and hear him in person. I consider how difficult it was for them to hear that he had to go away so that he could send the Counselor, the one who would never leave them.

If I had been in their shoes, I would have chafed at the change. I would have wanted him to stay with me. In human form, though, Jesus could be with only a limited number of people. However, in Spirit, he is unlimited. Although we won't be able to physically feel his touch until heaven, we can know his person, his words, and his teachings by listening to the Holy Spirit living inside of us.

If you get anything out of the lesson this week, let it be this:

He is no "it."
He is near you.
He will never leave you.
He lives inside of you.

How does knowing that the Holy Spirit is a "he" affect how you
   pray to him?

Why can't the world accept the Holy Spirit?

Why does Satan want you to believe that the Spirit is an "it," a thing
   to be used, discarded, or lost?

DAY 3

In the same way, the Spirit helps us in our weakness. We do not know what we
ought to pray for, but the Spirit himself intercedes for us with groans that words
cannot express.

Romans 8:26

Teach me to do your will, for you are my God; may your good Spirit lead me on
level ground.

Psalm 143:10

But the Counselor, the Holy Spirit, whom the Father will send in my name, will
teach you all things and will remind you of everything I have said to you.

John 14:26

Look again at the verses above and write four things the Spirit does
for us:

1. _____
2. _____
3. _____
4. _____

An "it" certainly couldn't do all those things, could it?

We've established that the Holy Spirit is a "he," a Holy He, to be exact. He is God in the Spirit, living inside of us. Let's compare the Holy Spirit to technology.

A couple of years ago, a friend of mine bought a PalmPilot. I've never seen him so pumped. He was completely psyched! He spent hours poring over the directions and learning how to enter information into the calendar, the address book, and other places. He constantly practiced and finally mastered how to use his pocket stylus pen. My friend learned a whole new language devoted to his PalmPilot. Words like *menu hack*, *Zip files*, *Memo Pad*, *palmtops*, and *ActiveSync* fluently rolled off his tongue in no time.

He learned how to enter appointments into his beloved PalmPilot, which elicited a series of friendly staccato beeps to warn him of an impending meeting. The amazing PalmPilot reminded him of phone numbers he couldn't commit to memory, and of birthdays in need of a card. For a mere $500, my friend acquired a kind of mini-secretary, something that could teach, guide, help, and remind at all times of the day. And it could even play solitaire!

And then one day, he dropped it.

No more stylus pen. No more friendly beeps. No more playing games with his other buddies who still had a working PalmPilot. My friend was devastated. And to be honest, a little lost.

There are some major similarities and differences between the Holy Spirit and a PalmPilot. The Holy Spirit leads us in the direction God would have us go. He reminds us of the truths found in Scripture and of lessons learned over the years. The Spirit teaches us right from wrong. He forms a bond between us and others who are filled with him. He warns us when we are in danger. And those who don't have the Holy Spirit are mystified by the lingo and the importance of him in our lives.

But unlike the PalmPilot, he can't break; we can't lose him; no one can steal him; he can't malfunction; his features can't go out of date; and his batteries won't run out of power. It's amazing that he is available to us 24/7; he longs to teach, lead, remind, and help.

Doesn't that make you psyched?

Which of the four things that the Spirit does for us means the most to you?

Why was it so important for God to send the Spirit?

Has there been a decision in your life you knew the Holy Spirit helped you make?

DAY 4

Do you not know that your body is a temple of the Holy Spirit, who is in you, whom you have received from God?

1 Corinthians 6:19a

But when he, the Spirit of truth, comes, he will guide you into all truth. He will not speak on his own; he will speak only what he hears, and he will tell you what is yet to come.

John 16:13

The Spirit of God has made me; the breath of the Almighty gives me life.

Job 33:4

Lots of people own exercise machines. Probably even more have memberships to athletic clubs. I, for one, am a proud owner of a treadmill. And no, I don't use it as an alternative for my closet.

However, statistics show that an alarming number of Americans do just that—or something like it. They have in their possession something that has the ability to transform their flab into fab, their chunky to hunky, bulky into burly. However, instead of utilizing their workout machine for good, they ignore it. They overlook it. They stack stuff on it. They sell it at a garage sale for a pittance. And they completely miss the benefits of owning health equipment.

Ignoring the Holy Spirit and not seeking his counsel daily is like owning an entire sports center full of the latest in exercise technology but never entering the gym. God promises to change us, to transform us into his likeness by the power of his Holy Spirit. However, in order for that to happen, God requires our attention, our involvement, our commitment.

I've often fantasized about how great it would be to have someone else exercise my body while I slept. I'd get all the benefits: no pain and all the gain! I could eat anything I wanted and send my body out to burn it all off. But I've come to the stark realization that there isn't anyone who can or will do this for me. If I want firmer calf muscles and a lower metabolism, it's up to me. If I want to bench-press my body weight and tone up for track tryouts, I need to form a plan and then execute it.

When we become Christians, we're not on autopilot. Our involvement isn't over. We can't just fill our minds with all kinds of junk and stuff and then expect the Spirit to sort it all out while we sleep. In order for the Holy Spirit to transform us, we need to seek his council; we need to study the Scriptures and ask for his discernment; we need to listen to his voice. He won't bellow over all the noise in our lives. We have to set aside some quiet time if we want to hear him.

God didn't send his Spirit to be ignored, to be overlooked, to be buried under a mound of activities and to-do lists. He sent his Spirit to render us holy, to spiritually turn our paunch into power, our blubber into brawn, our marshmallow into muscle. You get the idea.

He wants our participation. He doesn't need it. He requires it.

↑ Looking Up

Knowing your body is the temple of the Holy Spirit, how should you treat it?

In what ways have you seen God transform you toward his likeness?

What are some areas in your life that need a spiritual workout?

DAY 5

The man without the Spirit does not accept the things that come from the Spirit of God, for they are foolishness to him, and he cannot understand them, because they are spiritually discerned.

1 Corinthians 2:14

Those who live according to the sinful nature have their minds set on what that nature desires; but those who live in accordance with the Spirit have their minds set on what the Spirit desires. The mind of sinful man is death, but the mind controlled by the Spirit is life and peace.

Romans 8:5–6

And you also were included in Christ when you heard the word of truth, the gospel of your salvation. Having believed, you were marked in him with a seal, the promised Holy Spirit, who is a deposit guaranteeing our inheritance until the redemption of those who are God's possession—to the praise of his glory.

Ephesians 1:13–14

Ever been to a country where you don't speak the language?

A friend and I traveled to Europe one year. We rented a car to avoid the long lines and waits at the train stations and because we convinced ourselves we'd see more of Europe that way. OK, and because we were too old to get the cheap train passes.

We had a blast! We traveled through France, Germany, Austria, Switzerland, and Italy with our Citroën, our backpacks, our maps, and our handy-dandy dictionaries. Europeans, for the most part, are far more linguistically educated. In almost all the countries we traveled, someone knew at least a little English. And for those who didn't, we spoke louder, slower, and pointed a lot. This strategy worked just about everywhere.

Except in Stuttgart, Germany.

We were stuck in our Citroën, with a map, no one to point to, and an enormously complex roundabout roadway system. Our goal was to *leave* the beautiful city of Stuttgart, but instead, we kept coming right *back* to where we started—smack-dab in the middle of it!

After two painful hours of this, we decided to modify our tactic. Up to this point, we had been following signs that would lead us toward the town of Stadmitte and away from the clogged freeways of big-city Stuttgart.

It was at this point that I, the navigator, made an important discovery: the word "stadmitte" was not a city; it meant "city center." For the last two hours we had been driving in circles toward the very place we meant to leave!

Knowing the language would have helped. Knowing how a roundabout worked would have helped as well. Going through life without the translating power of the Holy Spirit is like traveling to a foreign country without an interpreter.

Don't believe me? Just try and explain the wonders of God, the mysteries of the Trinity, the awesomeness of the Spirit to an unbeliever. They won't get it. Not until they've experienced the indwelling of God.

His Holy Spirit is described in Ephesians 1:13–14 as a seal, a mark of ownership of God. He recognizes us because he has set us apart from those who on their own are incapable of understanding his ways.

I looked up the definition of *recognize*. Here's what I found:

1 : to acknowledge formally: as . . . to admit as being one entitled to be heard . . . **2 :** to acknowledge or take notice of in some definite way: as . . . to acknowledge acquaintance with <*recognize* a neighbor with a nod> **3 a :** to perceive to be something or someone previously known

Cool, huh?

Some people try to communicate with God without his Spirit; they talk louder, thinking that if they yell at God, he will make more sense to them. Some try to become Christians by association—befriending someone else who knows the "language."

Don't make the same mistake. Allow God to mark you with his Holy Spirit; follow his voice and no other. When you find yourself going in circles and heading nowhere, look to him for direction. He's the only one who can get you back on the straight and narrow path.

Do you know anyone who is stuck on a spiritual roundabout, heading in the wrong direction without the Holy Spirit to guide them?

Is it possible to live the Christian life without the Holy Spirit?

What was the most important thing you learned about the Holy Spirit this week?

DAY 6

Now it is God who makes both us and you stand firm in Christ. He anointed us, set his seal of ownership on us, and put his Spirit in our hearts as a deposit, guaranteeing what is to come.

2 Corinthians 1:21–22

But the fruit of the Spirit is love, joy, peace, patience, kindness, goodness, faithfulness, gentleness and self-control. Against such things there is no law. . . . Since we live by the Spirit, let us keep in step with the Spirit. Let us not become conceited, provoking and envying each other.

Galatians 5:22–23, 25–26

Make every effort to keep the unity of the Spirit through the bond of peace. There is one body and one Spirit—just as you were called to one hope when you were called—one Lord, one faith, one baptism; one God and Father of all, who is over all and through all and in all.

Ephesians 4:3–6

Billy and Mario have always been good friends, but they've always attended different churches. Neither will go to the other's church. Mario thinks Billy's church is too tame; Billy doesn't really like all of the yelling and dancing that goes on during the worship services at Mario's church. Even though they don't like each other's churches too much, they still get along. They've always gotten along.

Today, Mario and Billy didn't get along. It happened on the way home.

You're driving, and your friend Kim is in the passenger seat; Billy and Mario are sitting in the back having a mildly heated discussion about the Bible when Mario says, "I think that when the Holy Spirit comes on you, everything about you changes—especially the way you pray."

Billy looks confused. "What in the heck does that mean?"

"You know, the way you pray. Your prayer language. When the Holy Spirit baptizes you with power, he gives you a prayer language that only he understands."

"That's nuts," Billy responds. "There's no such thing as a prayer language. Ridiculous!"

The tension in the car mounts, and Mario retorts, "Whatever. It says in the Bible that the Holy Spirit gives us a prayer language. If you don't believe that, you're not reading the Word, and you're not living your life fully as a believer. You're way off base."

You look at Kim. She rolls her eyes as if to say, "Oooh boy."

"Are you calling me wrong?" Billy says. "You're the one who babbles when you pray. You're the idiot who looks like a freak when you pray."

You're driving along, hoping that Billy and Mario don't get physical. And you're wondering what it really means to have the Holy Spirit in your life. You're not sure it means being a babbler, but you're not convinced that it means you have to walk around like a boring believer either.

What does it mean to have the Holy Spirit in you? How can you help Billy and Mario better understand the Holy Spirit?

↑ Looking Up

Based on your study this week, what evidence is seen when the Holy Spirit lives inside a person?

To what Scripture would you direct Mario and Billy to help them better understand the Holy Spirit?

How does it affect the kingdom of God when believers argue and fight over issues like the indwelling of the Holy Spirit?

DAY 7

It does not, therefore, depend on man's desire or effort, but on God's mercy.

Romans 9:16

But thanks be to God that, though you used to be slaves to sin, you whole-heartedly obeyed the form of teaching to which you were entrusted. You have been set free from sin and have become slaves to righteousness.

Romans 6:17–18

In you, O LORD, I have taken refuge; let me never be put to shame; deliver me in your righteousness. Turn your ear to me, come quickly to my rescue; be my rock of refuge, a strong fortress to save me. Since you are my rock and my fortress, for the sake of your name lead and guide me.

Psalm 31:1–3

As believers, we are not in control of our lives. Yet we are told in the Scriptures to be self-controlled, giving up control of our lives to the one who already has the control in the first place. (Try saying that three times fast.)

Surrender is one of the most difficult things we can do. Submission to another rubs our little independent selves the wrong way. Face it—we're all control freaks at heart. Giving God all of us, and allowing him to control everything we are and everything we do, involves a daily giving over of our will, our desires, our plans. But make no mistake about it: God in his sovereign wisdom allows us the privilege of making this choice. Because he has already chosen us as his children.

Whoa, I know. That is a topic for a series of books all by itself. Let's break it down to a more manageable chunk. Try this activity:

[Read through all the directions before getting started!]

Put on two blindfolds. The top blindfold represents your will; the bottom blindfold represents your humanity. Allow a responsible adult to lead you to their car. Get in the drivers' seat and ask your partner to get in the passenger side. Then tell them to give you the keys and inform them that you're going to take a drive and that you're relying on them for good navigation.

I'm guessing you'll hear responses like "Fat chance," "Nice try," "Not on your life," or "What does this have to do with Bible study?"

After listening to their protests, reassure them and remove one of the blindfolds. Admit that you're not fully in control and that you'll be listening extra carefully to their directions, plus you will probably be able to see a teeny bit through the blindfold.

Hopefully they won't actually hand over the keys—because driving while blindfolded is like trying to maneuver your life without the Holy Spirit. Yes, you're in the drivers' seat and you have the keys, but you don't have the ability to see the dangers up ahead; you don't have the necessary tools to make the best, safest decisions; you don't *really* have control.

Spiritually speaking, even if you were to hand over the top blindfold—your will—the fact is you still have the second blindfold in place; this side of heaven you can never be rid of your humanity. Whether you believe it or not, as a human being your vision is severely impeded; you are a physical being surrounded by the spiritual. Only the Holy Spirit has the ability to see the dangers all around you.

So God asks you to give up control to the one who already has control in the first place. Not because he's a control freak, but because he loves you and wants to protect you from being broadsided by your own actions.

↑ Looking Up

What have you learned about your need for the Holy Spirit from this activity?

Using what you've learned from this illustration, how would you explain the importance of the Holy Spirit to your best friend?

How can you apply what you've learned and the truth you've discovered from Scripture about this topic?

WHY SHOULD I TALK TO GOD?

DAY 1

And pray in the Spirit on all occasions with all kinds of prayers and requests. With this in mind, be alert and always keep on praying for all the saints.

Ephesians 6:18

Answer me when I call to you, O my righteous God. Give me relief from my distress; be merciful to me and hear my prayer.

Psalm 4:1

This is the confidence we have in approaching God: that if we ask anything according to his will, he hears us.

1 John 5:14

It's been a long week. Weeks this long and difficult are both unfair and flat-out cruel. Three exams. A fight with a close friend. Yelled at by the coach. It's been too much.

You wander into the living room and notice your father reading a book on the couch. His glasses sit perched on the end of his nose, his brow furrowed in concentration. Even though he's an imposing 6 feet 4 inches tall, everything about him is inviting and comforting; from his favorite blue sweatshirt you gave him for Christmas last year down to his green holey socks.

You long for his wisdom, for his hug, for his understanding. As you cautiously approach, your dad closes his book, sets his glasses on the coffee table, and flashes you a friendly smile. "Hey, kiddo!"

"Dad . . . umm, can we . . . I know I'm getting a little old for this, but . . . ?"

Your dad nods at you with a "Get up here" look. And you do.

Your dad's lap has always been one of those safe places. Sometimes it's been the only safe place. Doesn't matter how old you are. Since you were small, you'd climb up, work your face into his neck, close your eyes, and forget.

This moment is familiar, and it feels good. The older your dad gets, the more comfortable he feels. And it doesn't matter that you're old enough to think this is kooky—your dad's lap is the best medicine for your awful week.

"Dad, it's been an awful week. Coach yelled at me. I know I failed one of my exams. I'm mad at Shelly, and I miss her."

You can feel your dad's chest expand with each breath. His strong arms make you feel safe. A bomb could go off right now, but you'd be okay in your dad's embrace.

"I know. It's tough, eh? I've been there. It'll be okay. I promise."

"School sucks."

"I know." Your dad's words are as steady as his breathing. As strong as his arms.

"I have no idea how I'm going to pull a C in chemistry."

"We'll work on it together."

"I'm confused about what I'm doing after graduation."

"Let's look at your options. I'll help you make a list."

"What should I do about Shelly?"

"Why don't you call her?"

Just like that. In quick succession, your father lovingly and gently listens to your problems and helps to bring them down from mountains to molehills. You wish you would have gone to him a few days ago instead of worrying yourself into insomnia and a stomachache. You make a promise to yourself that next time you will go right to your dad, knowing he will be there and will help you in any situation.

↑ Looking Up

All earthly fathers let their children down. How does the father in this story compare with your expectations with God?

In what ways do you think you've let God down?

What would it be like to have a father who never failed you, who never let you down?

DAY 2

God is our refuge and strength, an ever-present help in trouble.

Psalm 46:1

I lift up my eyes to the hills—where does my help come from? My help comes from the LORD, the Maker of heaven and earth.

Psalm 121:1–2

I urge you, brothers, by our Lord Jesus Christ and by the love of the Spirit, to join me in my struggle by praying to God for me.

Romans 15:30

You just can't write a devotion for teens about praying for God's help without mentioning the opening lyrics from the classic Beatles' song "Help!" They talk about needing somebody, anybody. I'm serious—they pretty much say everything, don't they?

We all need help—but not just from anybody. From God.

Many of us struggle asking for help. The reason? Pride. We live in a society where tough, strong, independent individuals are admired and looked up to. People who need help are seen as weak, insecure, inadequate—the bottom dwellers of the food chain.

How often do you ever watch movies where the main character shows any sign of weakness or asks for help? The messages from television, movies, books, magazines, radio, our culture, are loud and strong:

- You can do anything you set your mind to
- Just do it
- Be all that you can be
- If it is to be, it's up to me

This has been true for male characters in movies and television for years, but the trend is starting to shift toward women as well. In fact, I bet if you closed your eyes right now, you could picture some tough actor chick beating the hooey out of everyone within range—all without breaking a nail or a sweat.

It comes as a shock when we realize that we *can't* do anything we set our minds to. That there are some things we simply *can't* do. That I *am* being all I can be, and quite frankly, it's not too impressive. That if it is to be, it's up to GOD.

Be encouraged. If you are working through this book, you've discovered a few things about God and yourself. You are more than likely ready to admit the fact that you are a mortal being in need of an immortal God.

Let's set aside our pride this week as we learn to come before the Lord in prayer, asking for his help in our times of trouble.

List three things you'd like God's help with:

- _____

- _____

- _____

↑ Looking Up

What are some ways you have tried and failed in your own efforts?

How difficult is it for you to ask someone for help? (1 = easy, 10 = almost impossible)

Why is it important to recognize our failings, our need for help?

DAY 3

I pray that out of his glorious riches he may strengthen you with power through his Spirit in your inner being, so that Christ may dwell in your hearts through faith. And I pray that you, being rooted and established in love, may have power, together with all the saints, to grasp how wide and long and high and deep is the love of Christ.

Ephesians 3:16–18

Devote yourselves to prayer, being watchful and thankful.

Colossians 4:2

The LORD is near to all who call on him, to all who call on him in truth. He fulfills the desires of those who fear him; he hears their cry and saves them.

Psalm 145:18–19

I'm making a list and checking it twice. A prayer list, that is.

I wonder how many of us have prayer lists stashed away in the recesses of our minds. Wish lists that we bring before God every once in a while, hoping that eventually he'll see things our way.

Have you ever heard someone say that God changed his mind about something? Don't believe it. He can't. Really. His decisions are perfect every time. Don't believe me? Check out these verses:

I the LORD do not change. (Malachi 3:6)

Every good and perfect gift is from above, coming down from the Father of the heavenly lights, who does not change like shifting shadows. (James 1:17)

Ever tried to pray so that God will change his mind? That he will alter his predetermined will for your life? That somehow, with all your begging and pleading, you've finally worn him down and he'll just give in? It ain't gonna happen.

"So what's the point of prayer if God won't change his mind?" you may be asking.

The point is that prayer changes *you*.

We pray to God so he will transform us, grow us, change us—not the other way around. When we talk to God, and listen to God, we become more like him.

Ever been around someone with an accent? I find it impossible not to start talking just like them before too long. Sometimes I even apologize, explaining that, no, I'm not making fun of them, I just can't help it. I've got friends all over the world, so my tongue has gotten twisted in all sorts of different shapes over the years.

With my Canadian friends, I say "aboot" and "eh?"

With my Southern friends, I say "y'all."

With my Michigan friends, I start talking about "soda" with a cute little nasal intonation on the *O*.

And with my East Coast friends, I just rag on the Yankees.

My speech just naturally tends to flow toward my companions. The same is true with prayer. The more you talk to God, the more you will hear him. The more you hear him, the more you will be changed into his likeness. It's impossible to experience the wonder and person of God without being changed.

Don't look at prayer as a big Christmas list. Prayer is so much more than that. Yes, bring your requests to him (we just did it on Day 2), but bring them to him and leave them with him, knowing that he will make the best possible decision. Asking God for something isn't wrong—he wants us to ask him for things. And then he wants us to trust him with the answer.

Prayer may not be what you expected; it's a lot, lot more—eh?

↑ Looking Up

What are some prayers of yours God has answered yes to?

What are some prayers of yours God has answered no to?

Why is it important to realize that God cannot and will not be swayed by the fickleness and selfishness of people?

DAY 4

Help us, O God our Savior, for the glory of your name; deliver us and forgive our sins for your name's sake.

Psalm 79:9

The LORD has heard my cry for mercy; the LORD accepts my prayer.

Psalm 6:9

Give ear to my words, O LORD, consider my sighing. Listen to my cry for help, my King and my God, for to you I pray. In the morning, O LORD, you hear my voice; in the morning I lay my requests before you and wait in expectation.

Psalm 5:1–3

If we confess our sins, he is faithful and just and will forgive us our sins and purify us from all unrighteousness.

1 John 1:9

Busted!

Do you ever feel like that when your parents find out you've goofed up—again? Do you get tired of apologizing for the same old mistakes time after time? Do you find yourself thinking, "What is the point of apologizing? I'm just going to mess up again." Then you, my friend, are not alone. Far from it, in fact.

Take a moment and write down three things with which you have struggled in the past and asked for forgiveness numerous times.

* _____

* _____

* _____

OK, set the list aside for a moment; we'll come back to it later.

You know that little voice, the one that tells you that you've failed God for the last time and there's NO WAY he's going to forgive you this time? That's not the Holy Spirit, in case you're wondering. That's Satan. His plan from the beginning has been to keep you and God apart. He knows that he can't influence God. He knows God already provided a plan of reconciliation through the death and resurrection of his Son, Jesus Christ.

So Satan has moved on to you and your insecurities about being busted—again. He knows that if he parades all your past mistakes right in front of your nose, your first instincts are to go running for cover rather than coming clean with the Lord.

That's where prayer comes in. When we pray to God, explaining to him how we goofed (again), he is not surprised. He's not shocked. Remember way back in Week 1, Day 1? God knows everything. Don't give up on his ability to forgive and change you. Lay your sins before him every day, trusting him to forgive and work through your heart.

Now look at the list above again. On the following lines, write a thank-you note to God for his forgiveness for those specific three areas. Thank him ahead of time for the changes he is going to make in your life regarding those sins.

- _____

_____

- _____

_____

- _____

_____

Does that mean you won't struggle with these particular sins ever again? Nope. We will suffer from the effects of sin until we get to heaven, my friend. But we don't have to suffer under the guilt of sin for another second. Jesus paid for your sin. He longs to forgive you, to release you from the burden of blame. Don't focus on your past mistakes; keep your eyes forward, toward the cross.

And if Satan tries to heap loads of guilt on your shoulders again? Tell him he's busted! And you're not falling for it anymore.

↑ Looking Up

Why is seeking forgiveness such an important part of our prayer life?

Why does Satan love it when we're afraid to approach God?

How many times have you gone to God for forgiveness this week?

DAY 5

Call to me and I will answer you and tell you great and unsearchable things you do not know.

Jeremiah 33:3

My sheep listen to my voice, I know them, and they follow me. I give them eternal life and they shall never perish; no one can snatch them out of my hand.

John 10:27–28

From one man he made every nation of men, that they should inhabit the whole earth; and he determined the times set for them and the exact places where they should live. God did this so that men would seek him and perhaps reach out for him and find him, though he is not far from each one of us.

Acts 17:26–27

He is not far from each one of us.

There are times when it feels like God is millions of miles away from me. And there are times when it seems as if he's sitting right next to me. I find it cool to know that God created me in a specific family, city, county, country, and year, all of which operate together to pull me closer to him.

Everything about me is created with the purpose of drawing me toward him, of showing me how much I need him, and of demonstrating how much he loves me. The same is true of you.

Take a minute and answer some questions:

Name _____

Age _____ Birthday _____ Gender _____

Born in [city, state, country] _____

Family members _____

_____

_____

(Don't worry, I won't ask about your weight.)

Looks a little like the forms you fill out at the doctor's office, doesn't it? The above information is not random. It's not just an accident. Taken together, the data about you forms a perfect access code straight to God.

The wonderful thing about God is that he won't put you on hold. And he doesn't have call waiting. And he won't hang up on you, run out of batteries, or lose connection with his satellite.

God is available, ready and waiting for YOU. Parents are busy; teachers are busy; coaches are busy; friends are busy; heck, even pastors are busy. But God is always ready and willing to listen, to talk.

OK, he doesn't often speak out loud (but who's to say he can't—he IS God). He talks to us through his Word, the Bible. He communicates to us through the words of others. And he speaks to our hearts through prayer.

He speaks words of comfort, words of wisdom, words of instruction. He speaks words of love and correction. The Psalms are an excellent place to go for examples of praying and listening to God. David, the one to whom many of the Psalms are attributed, prayed to God in a variety of situations. At times he cried out in anger or in despair. David sang joyfully to God; and he prayed with tears of repentance at times as well.

David lived in Israel around 1050 BC. He was the son of Jesse, a shepherd. He was the youngest and the smallest of seven brothers. David ruled Israel as king from 1010 BC to 970 BC. All his personal information was known ahead of time by God, the one who wanted to know and talk with David. His birthday and address were no mistake. Neither are yours.

He's waiting . . .

Are you perhaps ready to reach out for him?

↑ Looking Up

Have you ever heard God speak to you (through Scripture, in your heart, through others)?

How do others respond when you tell them that God spoke to you?

What are some things you'd like to talk with God about?

DAY 6

I call on you, O God, for you will answer me; give ear to me and hear my prayer.

Psalm 17:6

So I say to you: Ask and it will be given to you; seek and you will find; knock and the door will be opened to you. For everyone who asks receives; he who seeks finds; and to him to knocks, the door will be opened.

Luke 11:9–10

Is any one of you in trouble? He should pray. Is anyone happy? Let him sing songs of praise. Is any one of you sick? He should call the elders of the church to pray over him and anoint him with oil in the name of the Lord.

James 5:13–14

"God, I'm hurting. Mom and Dad won't stop fighting. Mom sounds angry. Dad says he's leaving."

"God, I'm lonely. Bill broke up with me and now I don't have anyone to talk to. All of our friends are taking his side, and I'm all by myself. I'm lonely."

"God, all I want to do is get drunk and forget how much of a geek I am. I don't want to drink, but I don't know if I can stop myself."

"God, I hate myself. It feels a little better when I cut my wrists, but not better enough. I want to die."

"God, my life has no direction."

"God, I LOVE Erica. She doesn't know I exist. Help her see that she really does love me."

"God, help!" "God, please . . ." "God—I need you!"

God has a lot of work to do, doesn't he? Imagine all of the stuff God hears from us. Do you think that God ever says,

"ENOUGH!"

Do you think he takes an hour off from listening? Do you suppose that God ever just wants a break? Have you ever pictured yourself in God's shoes?

Let's pretend for a brief moment that you're God. You have the ability to hear what people say when they pray. You also have the ability to talk back, and the people who are talking to you will know and hear your voice when you speak.

What will you say?

How will you say it?

Will you solve their problems?

How?

Being God can't be easy. So, let's reverse the question.

What does God say to you?

How does he say it?

Will he solve all of your problems?

How?

Feels much better being on this side of things, doesn't it? Spend some time this week talking to God about the answers to those questions. Remember that God can handle any question you throw at him; he isn't intimidated or frustrated or stressed out or too busy. Go to him; talk with him; climb up in his lap if you want to.

↑ Looking Up

What are some common misconceptions about prayer?

What are some things you've learned about prayer this week?

Why do you think some people refuse to bring their questions, concerns, and problems to God?

DAY 7

The voice of the LORD is powerful; the voice of the LORD is majestic.

Psalm 29:4

And everyone who calls on the name of the LORD will be saved; for on Mount Zion and in Jerusalem there will be deliverance, as the LORD has said, among the survivors whom the LORD calls.

Joel 2:32

For there is no difference between Jew and Gentile—the same Lord is Lord of all and richly blesses all who call on him, for, "Everyone who calls on the name of the Lord will be saved."

Romans 10:12–13

You know, talking to God can feel really tough sometimes. There are times when we try to sit and talk out loud or silently to him, and we feel silly, or we feel like our prayers are bouncing off the ceiling. Sometimes it can feel too difficult to talk to him.

I think that when it's difficult to talk to God, sometimes we need to renew our commitment to talk to him. Think about it like this. Say you and your dad haven't talked for a long time. Eventually, one of you breaks the silence and makes the first move to talk to the other. I think that often we need to find moments or places where we can sit and talk with God. I think that sometimes we need to be the ones who break the silence and take the first step to talk with him. To do that, try this:

Find a place in your house where you're really comfortable. Any place, including your bed or a couch or a closet, will work. Next, make sure that you have a pencil and a piece of paper with you.

Get comfortable and imagine that you're sitting next to God. Imagine that the two of you aren't talking. Instead, imagine that you're just quietly sitting together. Imagine how it might feel sitting next to the Creator of the universe.

Now begin to imagine the things you might say to him. As you imagine, write whatever comes to mind. If you imagine him saying anything, write that too. Keep track of the whole conversation as you imagine it. When you've sat and written down everything that you can think of, take time to read what you wrote.

What kind of a conversation would you have? What things do you think he'd say to you? What might you reveal to him? What would happen to your prayer life if you viewed it not like some kind of have-to thing every Christian did, but instead thought of it as an opportunity to sit next to your heavenly Father and tell him everything.

For the next week, spend at least fifteen minutes each day imagining that you're sitting next to God. Make sure you tell him all the small details of your life. He already knows everything, but sometimes it's good to experience his presence and let him know that you know he cares.

⬆ Looking Up

What have you learned about talking to God from this activity?

Using what you've learned from this illustration, how would you explain the importance of communicating with God to your best friend?

How can you apply what you've learned and the truth you've discovered from Scripture about this topic?

WHY SHOULD I DEFEND MY FAITH?

DAY 1

And you also must testify, for you have been with me from the beginning.

John 15:27

Timothy, my son, I give you this instruction in keeping with the prophecies once made about you, so that by following them you may fight the good fight, holding on to faith and a good conscience. Some have rejected these and so have shipwrecked their faith.

1 Timothy 1:18–19

Be on your guard; stand firm in the faith; be men of courage; be strong.

1 Corinthians 16:13

Fighting the good fight.

Umpteen number of battles have been waged over the centuries. Huge wars have been fought over issues such as land, money, boundaries, slavery, power, hate, and revenge. The causes vary as much as the people themselves. The individuals responsible for those wars had only one thing in common: a passion for their cause.

These military leaders were not content to simply have a passion—they needed to do something about it, knowing that their side was in danger of defeat. It's frightening to think how history would have been altered had the allies not combined forces against Adolf Hitler. Nazism was an evil that needed to be crushed; simply sitting back and merely having an opinion about it was not an option in 1942.

The battles for belief that we fight today are much different in scope and brutality than that of World War II. However, they are just as vital, because they involve matters of eternal significance—the difference between life and death.

In order to stand up for your faith, you have to have a passion for your beliefs; you have to know in your heart that what you believe about Jesus is right. Do you have a passion for Jesus? Are you moved to proclaim the truth of his salvation because you know the risks that

Why Should I Defend My Faith?

are at stake? If you realize the urgency of defending your faith, you also know that having a silent opinion is not an option.

The truth is, if you don't stand up for what you believe in, one or possibly both of these things will happen:

1. The "other side" will win. Satan wants to keep as many people from the gates of heaven as he can. Do you have a passion to share the Good News with the people around you? Being obedient to God and gently leading a person to Christ is the most important thing you will ever do. Don't let Satan cheat you out of that blessing.

2. Your silence or inaction will result in you being perceived as agreeing with the other side. Not saying a word in defense of your beliefs communicates volumes to those around you.

Let's take a look at the "good fight" this week by looking into the Bible for some good examples of how, when, and why to defend our faith.

↑Looking Up

What are some things you are passionate about?

What is the difference between defending your faith and attacking others with your faith?

Why does Satan love our silence?

DAY 2

Finally, be strong in the Lord and in his mighty power. Put on the full armor of God so that you can take your stand against the devil's schemes. For our struggle is not against flesh and blood, but against the rulers, against the authorities, against the powers of this dark world and against the spiritual forces of evil in the heavenly realms.

Ephesians 6:10–12

But the Lord is faithful, and he will strengthen and protect you from the evil one.

2 Thessalonians 3:3

Contend, O Lord, with those who contend with me; fight against those who fight against me.

Psalm 35:1

It's not about you.

Author Rick Warren begins his book *The Purpose Driven Life* with those very significant words. And he's right; it's not about us. The battle belongs to the Lord; he wages war against his enemy, the devil. Although you can't see the supernatural world, make no mistake that it exists, each side defending its position until the end.

Knowing that you're not alone and that you need not take Satan's attacks personally helps you to keep perspective. God doesn't expect you to single-handedly deliver the devil to him on a plate (breathe a big sigh of relief!). Rather, God promises to come alongside us, to equip us, and to encourage us.

The most encouraging aspect of this whole spiritual warfare thing is that the book of Revelation at the back of the Bible gives us the ending. Here's the spoiler for ya: God wins, hands down! Satan and all his demons will be forever defeated by the all-powerful, mighty, sovereign Lord. Just knowing that takes a little bit of the edge off, doesn't it?

The fact that it's a SUPERNATURAL battle should also chill us out a little when we're confronted about our faith. It may be difficult to remember, but we need to try: It is not us being attacked; it's God. It's not our friends attacking; they're listening to the lies of Satan.

Although we need to stand up for our beliefs and for our faith, there's no need to go on a rampage. The European Crusades of the eleventh century are a good example of a passionate faith gone amuck.

A group of zealous Britains, Frenchmen, and Italians joined forces with the intent to purge Christianity of all that was false and reclaim the Holy Land from the "Barbarian Turks." The European Christians versus the Muslims in the Middle East. Their symbol: a cross sewn onto the front of their tunics. Their device of persuasion: a sword.

All told, the Crusades lasted about 250 years. Hundreds of thousands of innocents were murdered in the name of Jesus Christ. In their passion, the "soldiers of the cross" killed anyone they assumed was not a Christian. As a result, thousands of Muslims were slaughtered, and many Christians and Jews were killed along with them.* Some sources show that around 150 Jewish communities were destroyed by the Crusaders. Christianity earned a violent reputation that, in some areas of the world, persists today.**

Misplaced passion, that's for sure. We as believers are *not* on a crusade.

There's a big difference between exacting vengeance on our enemies and teaching them truths from the Word of God.

And no, it's not about us; it's about the battle between good and evil, heaven and hell, God and Satan.

Whose side are you on?

↑ Looking Up

How does getting angry and yelling about your faith actually hurt the cause of Christ?

What are some things you can do when you find yourself getting out-of-control angry with a non-Christian?

Can you think of someone in your life who has demonstrated standing firm in their faith while maintaining their dignity and control?

* "Medieval Crusades," http://www.medievalcrusades.com/, accessed November 28, 2004.
** Ray Vander Laan, "Follow the Rabbi," http://community.gospelcom.net/Brix?pageID= 1594, accessed November 28, 2004.

DAY 3

I am not ashamed of the gospel, because it is the power of God for the salvation of everyone who believes: first for the Jew, then for the Gentile.

Romans 1:16

Give thanks to the LORD, call on his name; make known among the nations what he has done.

Psalm 105:1

Sing to the LORD a new song; sing to the LORD, all the earth. Sing to the LORD, praise his name; proclaim his salvation day after day.

Psalm 96:1–2

It's a little uncomfortable to admit how embarrassed I was by my parents when I was your age. I thought they were *so* dorky and uncool. My dad actually started teasing me by rolling his eyes and saying with a lame British accent, "Oh, *Faaather*!"

They are great parents; they were great in the '80s too. They treated me nicely, disciplined me firmly but not over the top. They were younger than all my friends' parents were, so they definitely had that going for them. They took my sisters and me to Disneyland three times, let me go (occasionally) to school dances, and even gave me a modest clothing allowance to pick out my own clothes.

Why was I so embarrassed by them?

Probably because ragging on your parents was the cool thing to do. Or because at home I was still treated like a kid (which I was). Or more likely because I was so insecure at the time, it made me feel a little better knowing that at least I was cooler than someone—anyone!

I wonder how it made them feel. After all their sacrifice, love, and hard work on my behalf, I treated them with disdain in front of my friends. They never said anything to me about how my verbal jabs hurt them.

However, when I went away to college, I realized something: I missed them! I appreciated them! My mom said she cried when I phoned her to tell her how sorry I was about being embarrassed by them and how much I loved them. These days my parents and I have a wonderful relationship; I finally see how blessed I am to have been given such parents.

I wonder how God feels when we're too embarrassed to share about him with others. Way too often, we're so busy keeping track of how others see us, we neglect God, and our faith in his Son, Jesus Christ.

Considering all he's done for us, we should be bursting at the seams to tell everyone around us how AWESOME he is! Instead, we're subdued, quiet, cool.

Take a minute and write down three things about God you're thankful for:

- _____
- _____
- _____

I bet you could think of even more if I gave you the space. Try not to let your friends' perceptions and opinions diminish the excitement you have for God. It's time to set the *cool* factor aside. If you don't, you'll regret it someday.

It might even embarrass you to admit it.

↑ Looking Up

Have you ever embarrassed someone else with your actions? How did it make you feel?

Was Jesus ever embarrassed about who he was and about who he represented?

Why do you think we are so concerned with what others think about us?

DAY 4

But in your hearts set apart Christ as Lord. Always be prepared to give an answer to everyone who asks you to give the reason for the hope that you have. But do this with gentleness and respect.

1 Peter 3:15

But the plans of the Lord stand firm forever, the purposes of his heart through all generations.

Psalm 33:11

Then I said to you, "Do not be terrified; do not be afraid of them. The Lord your God, who is going before you, will fight for you, as he did for you in Egypt, before your very eyes, and in the desert. There you saw how the Lord your God carried you, as a father carries his son, all the way you went until you reached this place."

Deuteronomy 1:29–31

As I was preparing for bed one night recently, I found a large chunk of blonde hair in the bathroom on the counter.

I do not have blonde hair.

In fact, the only person in our family who does have blonde hair is our five-year-old little girl.

Noticing a pair of scissors positioned conspicuously close to the hunk of hair, I made the logical conclusion and went hunting for the flashlight. Not wanting to wake her, I spent the next ten minutes probing through her sleepy head with the flashlight, trying to locate the inevitable bald patch.

The next morning, I confronted her with the scissors, the hunk of hair, and a no-nonsense, what-in-world-were-you-thinking lecture. Realizing the jig was up, she confessed to the crime. When asked why, her response was a pitiful, "I couldn't help it! It was just soooo much fun!"

Let's forget the "crime" context and look at her response again. These are the very words God longs to hear when questioned about why you courageously stood up for your faith, for why you proclaimed the greatness of his sacrifice, the wonder of his love.

Are you having fun as a Christian? Do you have the joy spoken of in Acts 14:17; Isaiah 55:12; and Romans 15:13? When asked about your beliefs do you jump in with enthusiasm only to say later, "Wow, I just couldn't help myself—it was just soooo much fun!"

OK, I know, life is always going to have its little ups and downs. God doesn't mean for us to put on a fake façade of flawlessness, to be the Jesus freak cheer squad.

But oh, how he wants us to enjoy him. To enjoy him so much that we can't help it—we can't wait to spread the Good News to others.

Standing up for your faith can be hard, embarrassing, uncomfortable, and even a little dangerous at times. But I hope you also experience the times of joy, the little glimpses of how God uses us to share with others, and then see how he changes their lives.

Spend some time in prayer this week, asking God for an opportunity to joyfully share your faith with someone.

↑ Looking Up

Do you know Christians who are always crabby and grumpy? What kind of an impact do you think they're making for Christ?

Can you think of someone you'd like to share some supernatural joy with?

Who is the one who LOVES to rob us of our joy?

DAY 5

All the prophets testify about him that everyone who believes in him receives forgiveness of sins through his name.

Acts 10:43

By standing firm you will gain life.

Luke 21:19

But the Lord stood at my side and gave me strength, so that through me the message might be fully proclaimed and all the Gentiles might hear it. And I was delivered from the lion's mouth. The Lord will rescue me from every evil attack and will bring me safely to his heavenly kingdom. To him be glory for ever and ever. Amen.

2 Timothy 4:17–18

Besides Jesus, which Bible character are you most looking forward to meeting in heaven? Moses? Elijah? Gideon? Esther? Mary? Peter? I love Old Testament history and can't wait to meet some of the Minor prophets and pick their brains for a bit.

However, the person I'm most interested in meeting (besides Jesus) is Paul. Paul, formerly known as Saul, wrote a lot of the New Testament books, like Romans, 1 and 2 Corinthians, Galatians, Ephesians, Philippians, Colossians, 1 and 2 Thessalonians, 1 and 2 Timothy, Titus, and Philemon. I know, he was a busy guy.

From chapter 8 in Acts to chapter 9, Saul transforms from the most vengeful oppressor of the faith to the most zealous defender of the faith, known thereafter as Paul.

What happened between chapters 8 and 9? What happened was an encounter with Jesus Christ on the road to Damascus. A divine meeting with the object of faith—the Messiah, the Anointed One, the Chosen One.

Paul was an educated Jew, a Pharisee who loved God's law. His enthusiasm for following the letter of the law permeated every aspect of his life. He began his own brutal crusade against the followers of Jesus, the Christians.

But once Paul realized the truth of Jesus's divinity, his devotion to the cause of Christ became unmatched. He is considered to be one of the greatest followers of Jesus Christ of all time.

Here's some of the fun things he experienced when standing up for his newfound faith in Jesus Christ (see 2 Corinthians 11):

He was . . .

Imprisoned
Flogged
Shipwrecked
Exposed to death
Beaten with rods
Stoned
Starved

Whew, kind of makes my life seem like one big picnic. But it shows me that God was with Paul and strengthened him to defend his faith in the face of brutality and death. I know he will strengthen me and give me the words as well. He stands by our side, just as he stood by all those Old and New Testament good ol' boys. I really can't wait to sit around and hear the stories. Of Rachel, Job, David, and Solomon. Of Joshua, Timothy, Jeremiah, and Nehemiah. Of Martha, Ezra, and . . .

↑ Looking Up

Have you had an encounter with Jesus Christ?

In what ways have you had to "suffer" for standing up for your faith?

How will God strengthen you for defending your faith?

DAY 6

Fight the good fight of the faith. Take hold of the eternal life to which you were called when you made your good confession in the presence of many witnesses.

1 Timothy 6:12

Do not be afraid of them; the Lᴏʀᴅ your God himself will fight for you.

Deuteronomy 3:22

First, I thank my God through Jesus Christ for all of you, because your faith is being reported all over the world.

Romans 1:8

The debate about how you can prove that God exists has been going on in your school for months. There are the atheists and their champion, Aletha; the Christians, many of whom are too intimidated by Aletha to come out in the open; and everyone in between, the onlookers to a long-running battle.

You and Aletha don't get along about anything. You're not friends at all, but she keeps popping up in your life. Aletha is the most outspoken atheist in your school. She leads group meetings and anti-Christian demonstrations, and she is always roaming the school with petitions she wants students to sign.

Aletha knows what she believes about atheism. She knows all of the proofs that Christians use to try to prove that God exists, and she has answers for every one. Aletha dislikes anyone who attends church and openly ridicules them. She antagonizes anyone who carries a Bible, anyone who wears a Christian T-shirt; she picks on people she knows attend youth group. In your school, public prayer isn't allwoed, and it's barely acceptable to wear Christian T-shirts. However, no one in the administration seems to care about Aletha and her friends wearing anti-Christian shirts or about her picking on Christians.

Today, Aletha decides to sit at your lunch table. She stares at you while you're in line. She watches where you sit, and now she sits just a few seats down. There's plenty of room in the lunchroom, so you figure you are her next target.

Soon, Aletha is joined by some of her atheist friends. She begins by making loud statements against Christians. How she doesn't like them. How they're all brainless and stupid. How they believe in a God that doesn't exist. After a long time, and many comments, Aletha turns to you and fires off a calculated line of questioning:

"So, Christian, how can you believe in an invisible God who allows people to hurt?

"How can you trust a God that lets people starve to death?

"Why would you believe in such an illogical lie?"

She finally stops to take a breath. All eyes are on you.

What will you say to Aletha?

↑ Looking Up

In this situation, the best way to begin is with a silent prayer. What are some things you could pray for Aletha? For yourself?

Remembering that God is with you and will fight this battle alongside you, what should your position be? Offensive and angry? Kind but firm? Emotional?

What are some verses you could use to answer Aletha's questions?

DAY 7

Let your conversation be always full of grace, seasoned with salt, so that you may know how to answer everyone.

Colossians 4:6

Do not be afraid or discouraged because of this vast army. For the battle is not yours, but God's.

2 Chronicles 20:15

The Lord is my strength and my shield; my heart trusts in him, and I am helped. My heart leaps for joy and I will give thanks to him in song.

Psalm 28:7

Defending your faith can feel like a constant war sometimes. If your parents aren't believers, you can feel at war with their beliefs. If your siblings aren't Christians, trying to live your beliefs in front of them can feel impossible. To get an understanding about how you can better defend what you believe, you're going to make a shield. Kind of.

Get a piece of paper and fold it in half, lengthwise, creating two columns. This is your shield.

On the left side of the shield, list all of the things that challenge your faith. Put things that tempt you, people who openly challenge your faith, etc.—maybe someone at your school, or a brother or sister, or your parents, or anyone who openly challenges your faith. You can also write down any media (movies or music) that you think are challenging to your beliefs. When you've written all of the things you can think of, step back and look at what you've written.

On the right side of the shield, put steps you can use to defend your faith. Each of these should be a direct defense for one of the things on the left side of the shield. For example, for one that reads "Explicit television shows," you might put "I promise to turn off the television." For one on the left that reads "When my older brother says God does not exist," you might put something like "I will be calm and explain one good reason why I know God exists." Think through a logical challenge to the things that challenge you.

When you're done with the shield, put it someplace where you'll see it each day. You might put it next to the door of your bedroom, or next to the front door of your house. Then, pray and ask God to help you use the things you thought up to stand strong and defend your faith. Each time you leave your room or your house, look at the shield. Think, *Which of these ways to defend my faith can I use tonight?* and *Which of these will I need while I am out with my friends?*

↑ Looking Up

What have you learned about defending your faith from this activity?

Using what you've learned from this illustration, how would you explain the importance of defending your faith to your best friend?

How can you apply what you've learned and the truth you've discovered from Scripture about this topic?

WEEK 11

WHY SHOULD I IMITATE JESUS?

DAY 1

But just as he who called you is holy, so be holy in all you do; for it is written: "Be holy, because I am holy."

1 Peter 1:15–16

Dear friend, do not imitate what is evil but what is good. Anyone who does what is good is from God. Anyone who does what is evil has not seen God.

3 John 11

My eyes are ever on the LORD, for only he will release my feet from the snare.

Psalm 25:15

Got a hero?

What does it take to be a hero? A human hero, that is. The ideal hero has to have accomplished something incredible in your eyes. They should also demonstrate integrity, boldness, and calmness in the midst of accomplishing their task.

Heroes don't have to be rich.

Heroes don't have to be famous.

Heroes don't have to be beautiful or handsome.

Heroes don't have to be powerful.

These days there are potential heroes in every corner of society. And, because each of us admires different qualities and accomplishments, each of us will undoubtedly have our own idea about what makes the perfect hero.

We imitate heroes, don't we? If you don't believe me, consider the costumes sold at Halloween or the millions of sports jerseys sold each year with different superstars' names on them. We seem to have an in-born need to imitate someone who's successful. We need these people to look up to and admire.

Do you have a hero? Someone you imitate? Can you name three people who are so important to you that you'd consider them heroes? They could be a parent, a teacher . . . anyone, really. Make a list of your top four below.

- _____
- _____
- _____
- _____

Setting aside our human heroes for a moment, let's consider Jesus Christ. He's really the perfect hero, the perfect person to imitate. In difficult situations, he acted perfectly. Faced with a threat on his life, he confronted his accusers. Upset over how God's house was being used, he took the appropriate action. Betrayed by a friend, he loved and forgave him.

This week we'll get to know Jesus as our Hero, and we'll learn how we can imitate him.

**Looking Up**

Have you had a hero let you down?

Has anyone ever looked up to you as a hero?

What are some characteristics you think are important for a hero to possess?

DAY 2

But as for me, I watch in hope for the Lord, I wait for God my Savior; and God will hear me.

Micah 7:7

Look at the nations and watch—and be utterly amazed. For I am going to do something in your days that you would not believe, even if you were told.

Habakkuk 1:5

But if from there you seek the LORD your God, you will find him if you look for him with all your heart and with all your soul.

Deuteronomy 4:29

"You can observe a lot just by watching."

This famous quote by Yogi Berra gets to the heart of imitating Jesus. Watching him, observing him, seeing him work all around us is what motivates us to emulate him.

In order to truly imitate someone, you have to spend a lot of time memorizing their movements, their actions, their words, their mannerisms. It's not an easy task, nor is it a quick one. When we apply this "watching" principal to Jesus, it's especially difficult since he's not physically in front of us. Think outside the box a little with me here. Try to come up with ways we can "watch" Jesus. Reread the Scripture verses above for help. To get your creative juices flowing, I'll get you started:

1. Read passages in the Old Testament and watch carefully for references to Jesus Christ (Psalms, Isaiah, etc.).*
2. Now move to the New Testament and look in one of the Gospels (Matthew, Mark, Luke, or John). Watch how Jesus treated people and handled situations.
3. Is there someone you know whose life has been drastically changed following their conversion to Christianity? By watching their transformation, you are watching Jesus at work.

* Check out Genesis 3:15; Psalms 22:14–18; 77:13–15; Isaiah 8:13–15; 33:22.

OK, now it's your turn:

4. _____

5. _____

It takes a lot of concentration to watch someone intently. Have you ever noticed how people watch television? Eyes glazed over, mouth hanging open, ears completely tuned in to the program and tuned out from everything else. Check out our list again; have you ever "watched" Jesus with the same intensity as when you're watching television? Probably not. More than likely, most of us haven't.

Why should we? Because in his Word, he has commanded us to watch—and be utterly amazed by what we will see. To be utterly amazed means to have our

eyes glazed over
mouths hanging open
ears tuned in to God alone

Have you ever walked out of the room for a second during your favorite TV show and then come back to find out you missed the most important part? It's such a bummer!

God doesn't want us to miss the most important part—Jesus. He knows that the only way we'll be able to come close to imitating him is to watch. And you know, you can observe a lot just by watching.

↑ Looking Up

Who in your life have you spent a lot of time watching?
What kinds of things do you watch for?
Are you willing to take some time this week to *really* watch Jesus?

DAY 3

Lift your eyes and look to the heavens: Who created all these? He who brings out the starry host one by one, and calls them each by name. Because of his great power and mighty strength, not one of them is missing.

Isaiah 40:26

Do not follow the crowd in doing wrong.

Exodus 23:2

When Jesus spoke again to the people, he said, "I am the light of the world. Whoever follows me will never walk in darkness, but will have the light of life."

John 8:12

Polyester pantsuits. Go-go boots. Tie-dye T-shirts. Bell bottoms. Tube tops. Stonewashed jeans. Leg warmers. JNCO jeans. Doc Martens.

What do these things have in common? They're fads, passing fashion—clothing styles that come and go in a whirlwind. Taken by themselves, it is difficult to see the value in these fashion fads. What made them so popular? Why would anyone wear leg warmers over their stonewashed jeans? Because *everyone* else was wearing them, of course.

In order to fit in, a lot of teen guys in the '80s wore bolo ties, Michael Jackson "Thriller" jackets, parachute pants, or pink paisley shirts (go ahead and shudder, it wasn't the best era in clothing). The girls wore things like roach clips, Bongo jeans, stirrup pants, bubble dresses, big blazers (with extra shoulder pads), big earrings, and most important—really, REALLY big hair. With lots of hair spray.

Oh, I know, you may assume that all the cool stuff we wear these days will never look dorky. Think again. Someday, the next generation will see pictures of you decked out in a trucker hat or pink fuzzy Ugg boots and ask, "*What* were you thinking?"

Fads are visual proof of the fact that we go through life imitating others, in both good and bad ways. Clothing fads aren't generally wrong—morally, that is. We could definitely argue about the fashion wrongness of a few particular items above. Our imitation isn't limited

Why Should I Imitate Jesus?

to the clothing rack, however. Behaviors are mimicked, as are mannerisms, language, and belief systems.

That's where Jesus comes in. The Bible says he's the same yesterday, today, forever (Hebrews 13:8). He is unaffected by the latest issue of *People* magazine. He is not a whim to be picked up and then dropped at the first sign of boredom. We imitate Christ because we are secure in his identity; we are secure in knowing that the characteristics that mark him as loving, kind, compassionate, forgiving, selfless will always be there.

Just think how difficult it would be if the foundation of your faith was variable; if it depended upon the fickle whims of the day. Just when you think you had gotten to know God, he decided to change, along with his requirements for salvation. It's ridiculous to imagine . . .

God: "Yes, I know that I said before that belief in my Son guaranteed salvation for eternity, but I'm kind of tired of that. Now, I'm thinking that if you shave your head and raise turkeys in the wilderness of northern Australia, then you could be saved for real." Not!

Imitate Jesus. He will never change. His sacrifice for you will never dim with time. And he will never require you to wear a polyester pantsuit.

↑ Looking Up

What are some of the fashion fads you have enjoyed over the years?

Are there some things in your life you wish wouldn't change so much?

What is the stability offered by God through faith in his Son?

DAY 4

I tell you the truth, anyone who has faith in me will do what I have been doing. He will do even greater things than these, because I am going to the Father.

John 14:12

My heart says of you, "Seek his face!" Your face, LORD, I will seek.

Psalm 27:8

"Come, follow me," Jesus said, "and I will make you fishers of men."

Matthew 4:19

When my children were babies, I couldn't keep my eyes off them. I was so in awe of them, of their mannerisms, their every movement. Once we had children, we had no reason to watch television anymore. Our evenings were spent watching them. Watching as they grew and developed. And watching how this growth occurred from their attempts at imitating us.

They imitated our walking, talking, laughing, tickling, and even our sneezing! I remember being in a restaurant one time when our two-year-old son waved the waiter over to our table.

"Man, excuse me, Mr. Man. I'm finished with my food. Please take away my plate."

We've definitely had more than our share of chuckles over our kids' rendition of adulthood. Why do they imitate us? Because they love, respect, admire, and need us. When I see them behaving kindly toward someone because they've watched and listened to me, I am thrilled; I am honored. And when they do it in public, I'm downright giddy.

Do you think God gets giddy over you and your behavior?

What do you think he says when he sees you

carrying groceries for an old woman to her car?

reading a bedtime story to your younger sister?

volunteering to help with Vacation Bible School?

Can't you just see him up in heaven saying, "Yup, that's my boy. That's my girl"?

Come and follow Jesus. Honor God with your actions. Your Father in heaven delights in seeing your growth. He loves to watch as you toddle through life imitating him. He loves you so much he can't keep his eyes off you.

↑ Looking Up

What are some ways you have imitated Christ in your life?

Have you done anything that you think made God a little giddy?

How do you show your love, admiration, and respect toward God?

DAY 5

You became imitators of us and of the Lord; in spite of severe suffering, you welcomed the message with the joy given by the Holy Spirit.

1 Thessalonians 1:6

Consider the blameless, observe the upright; there is a future for the man of peace.

Psalm 37:37

Follow my example, as I follow the example of Christ.

1 Corinthians 11:1

You are being watched. OK, maybe not at this *exact* moment, but in general, you truly are being watched.

By your brothers, sisters, or cousins—especially if they're younger than you

By your teachers

By your neighbors

By your peers

By anyone who knows you're a Christian

Why? Because they want to know if what you profess is genuine. If it's real. If it's lasting. If it makes a difference in how you treat others and live your life. I know, talk about pressure!

Thankfully, God doesn't send us out in the fishbowl alone. As we learned in Week 8, he equips us with his Holy Spirit and teaches us more about him along the way.

When we look to Christ and imitate him, we offer living examples of him to people who may never have another encounter with him again. We imitate Christ to show others how much he loves them and how much he longs to forgive them.

If we acted on our own, choosing not to watch and imitate Jesus, what would others see? Our anger, resentment, hostility, impatience, selfishness, pride. Ugh. Not exactly a glowing recommendation for Christianity, huh?

When we set aside our selves by fixing our eyes on Jesus, we can't help but imitate him. And that's what catches the eye of the watchers around us. Too often, as Christians we think we're supposed to argue others into the kingdom of God, like ruthless cattle drivers. Instead, we're supposed to lead them by example—not our own, but Jesus's.

Let's chill for a moment. Reflect on the beauty we see when we observe Jesus. Let's set our cattle prods down and take a good look at the things others see when they look at us, at our hearts. They want to know if our faith is real.

Is it?

↑ Looking Up

Who are some people you have imitated over the years?

Who are some people you think may be imitating you?

What do others see when they watch you?

Those who look to him are radiant; their faces are never covered with shame.

Psalm 34:5

Look to the LORD and his strength; seek his face always.

Psalm 105:4

Let us fix our eyes on Jesus, the author and perfecter of our faith, who for the joy set before him endured the cross, scorning its shame, and sat down at the right hand of the throne of God.

Hebrews 12:2

Micah's parents have been divorced since he was seven years old. With his dad out of the house and his mom always working to support the family, Micah didn't have anyone at home to look up to or to take care of him. He didn't have anyone to show him how to deal with life.

Micah's family does attend church on the weekends that his mom doesn't have to work. Unfortunately, because Micah's attendance is so irregular, he hasn't been able to make any real friends at church; he's the loner of the youth group, the one who sits by himself off to the side.

His youth pastor invites him out for lunch one day and asks him how life is going. Upset about his father leaving, angry that his mom has been forced to work, frustrated that he comes home from school to an empty house and an emptier refrigerator, Micah spills his guts.

"I'm angry. My parents don't love me. Our house feels empty; I'm all alone all the time. I hate school, church, my friends . . . and my life. I really hate my life!"

A little taken aback by Micah's outburst, the youth pastor asks gently, "Don't you have a good friend or a relative to help you out? Someone you look up to?"

Micah sighs. "I have no one to look up to."

"I know someone you could look up to. I know someone who could make you feel a lot better."

Micah stands up and says, "You know, I'm tired of hearing that. Jesus doesn't fix everything. He doesn't make every situation better. He doesn't heal all my hurts. If he did, my parents would be married and my life wouldn't feel so empty What's the point of having a role model who can't make my life better?"

↑ Looking Up

How would you help Micah learn the importance of imitating Jesus?

In what ways is Micah right about what Jesus does and doesn't do?

How does Micah have his definition of a role model a little screwed up?

DAY 7

May the God who gives endurance and encouragement give you a spirit of unity among yourselves as you follow Christ Jesus, so that with one heart and mouth you may glorify the God and Father of our Lord Jesus Christ.

Romans 15:5

Therefore, holy brothers, who share in the heavenly calling, fix your thoughts on Jesus, the apostle and high priest whom we confess.

Hebrews 3:1

But if anyone obeys his word, God's love is truly made complete in him. This is how we know we are in him: Whoever claims to live in him must walk as Jesus did.

1 John 2:5–6

How in the world are you supposed to imitate Jesus? You can't touch him. You can't see him. You don't know how he'd react to getting a

C in biology, and you're not aware of how he'd react to you getting grounded. The fact that Jesus lived 2,000 years ago makes it difficult to imitate him in every way. So, try this to get a better understanding about how to imitate Jesus.

Get a movie or music poster. If you don't have one, you can use the cover of a movie or CD you own. Pretty much any movie or music poster or picture will work. Whatever media pic you choose, it needs to be of something or someone you admire. When you've got your picture, think through what you know about the lead actor or lead singer. Ask yourself why you admire the actor or singer. For example, you might admire her real-life decision-making abilities, his bold stance in his lyrics, or you might admire something about the character he plays in the movie.

After you've thought for a bit, write those things that you admire on sticky notes and put them on the front of the picture. Think up as many things as you can and try and cover the poster with different admirable things.

Then ask yourself, what makes this person worth imitating? Why would people imitate this person's actions, attitude, or personality? What similarities are there between imitating a hero and imitating Christ?

Next, imagine that you're standing in front of a poster with the picture of Jesus on it. Ask yourself, what makes Jesus worth imitating? What make his actions, attitude, and personality worth imitating?

Turn the picture of the famous person over, and using the sticky notes, list the traits that you know about Jesus. For example, you might write "patient" or "enduring." Write one on each sticky note and put each one in a different place on the back of the poster. When you're done, look at the words you've written. Which of these words would be easy to imitate? Which ones would be difficult to imitate?

Put the picture in your room in a place where you'll see it every day. Each day when you pass the picture, reach around to the back and pull off one of the sticky notes. That day, do your best to imitate Jesus's personality trait that you've identified.

Here's the goal in all of this: Everyone has a hero, and we know all about those heroes from movies or their music. And, it's often difficult to imitate Jesus because he feels so removed from our daily lives. When we stop to consider the character traits of Jesus and look for these qualities in Scripture, we see the kind of hero we should be imitating.

↑ Looking Up

What have you learned about imitating Jesus from this activity?

Using what you've learned from this illustration, how would you explain to your best friend the importance of imitating Jesus?

How can you apply what you've learned and the truth you've discovered from Scripture about this topic?

WHY SHOULD I LIVE IT REAL?

DAY 1

Keep my commands and you will live; guard my teachings as the apple of your eye. Bind them on your fingers; write them on the tablet of your heart.

Proverbs 7:2–3

May our Lord Jesus Christ himself and God our Father, who loved us and by his grace gave us eternal encouragement and good hope, encourage your hearts and strengthen you in every good deed and word.

2 Thessalonians 2:16–17

So, if you think you are standing firm, be careful that you don't fall!

1 Corinthians 10:12

OK, so let's review.

Why should you . . . be honest with God? Be honest with others? Be honest with yourself? Be humble? Serve others? Carry your cross? Be discipled? Talk to God? Defend your faith? Imitate Jesus? Why do you need the Holy Spirit?

A faith that connects is a faith that's real, that's lived out every day. And living it real involves incorporating the answers to those questions into your life. Carefully, consistently, decisively, tenaciously, daily. If you skipped through a few chapters, I encourage you to back up the truck and pay careful attention to the Scripture and the lessons that need to be sifted through.

So, why do *you* think you need to live it real? (If you need to thumb through the first eleven chapters to help you answer, go for it.)

- _____
- _____
- _____
- _____
- _____

Living it real means having a genuine faith—one that is not pretend or put on for show. Someone whose faith is real is unsinkable in the midst of a storm. They may get a little wet and have doubts; they may even get a little seasick as they process through their grief, anger, and frustrations. But in the end, their faith stays afloat. Their belief in Jesus is anchored by the indwelling Holy Spirit of God.

Have you experienced any storms lately? Rest assured that if you haven't already, you will someday. Are you prepared to handle the waves of adversity and the winds of disappointment? Don't try to face them on your own. Remember Peter in Matthew 14:22–32?

Peter and the rest of the disciples were caught in the middle of a doozy of a storm on the Sea of Galilee. Try to picture it with me. The waves are crashing, the boat is rocking. Pretty soon they notice a disturbing sight—someone, or *something*, is walking toward them on the water. At first they cry out in fear (uh, wouldn't you, too?), but then Jesus calls out to them, "Take courage! It is I. Don't be afraid."

True to his delightfully impulsive nature, Peter replies, "Lord, if it's you, tell me to come to you on the water."

Jesus beckons him to follow, and Peter hops out of the boat and walks toward Jesus on the water. What an amazing experience! Unfortunately, it doesn't last long. His doubts and fears grab hold of him, and Peter begins to sink.

Jesus quickly comes to his rescue and says, "You of little faith, why did you doubt?"

OK, compared to me, Peter's faith was ENORMOUS. I'm not sure I could have gotten out of the boat. Jesus wanted Peter's complete trust in the middle of the storm, and he wants ours as well.

Go out this week in faith, trusting in Jesus to be your anchor—not just in the midst of the calm, but in the midst of the storm too. Be looking for him; be waiting for him. But when you behold him in his glory, don't be afraid, just follow him.

Would your friends and family describe your faith as "real living faith"?

Do you know someone who has demonstrated living it real in the midst of a storm?

Can you think of a time when you stepped out in faith like Peter, trusting Jesus in the middle of unbelievable circumstances?

DAY 2

I have fought the good fight, I have finished the race, I have kept the faith.

2 Timothy 4:7

We wait in hope for the LORD; he is our help and our shield. In him our hearts rejoice, for we trust in his holy name. May your unfailing love rest upon us, O LORD, even as we put our hope in you.

Psalm 33:20–23

We must pay more careful attention, therefore, to what we have heard, so that we do not drift away.

Hebrews 2:1

What type of runner are you? Long distance? Sprinter? Do you take great strides or do you shuffle along? Or maybe you prefer to sit in the grandstand, cheering on the other runners. Personally, I am not a runner—I'm a walker, and only on really good days.

My friend, Sheri, however, is a marathon runner. She is a looonnggg-distance runner, a 26.2-mile runner to be exact. And the bizarre part is that she loves it. She spends a good hour every day running. Every day. Without fail. Even with small children to raise, she always finds time to get away and run. I call her the Energizer Bunny behind her back—don't tell.

She has been training and running for so long that it is programmed into the very fiber of her being. If Sheri couldn't run, I think she would shrivel up and die. (I, on the other hand, would shrivel up and die if I couldn't eat chocolate.)

When Sheri ran in her first marathon a few years ago, I was so proud of her. After hearing about how she had accomplished one of her life goals by completing the race, I was thrilled for her and maybe a little jealous too. I was also a little in awe of her. I mean, how in the world does someone run for 26.2 miles?

They train for months. They practice. They sacrifice time. They work hard.

Living it real means completing the race set before you. It means living the life of faith with purpose and determination. It means spending a lifetime training under the tutelage of the Holy Spirit. It means practicing every day. It means sacrificing and working hard. Living it real means that if you didn't spend time with Jesus every day, you would shrivel up and die.

What type of a spiritual runner are you? Long distance? Sprinter? Do you take great strides or do you shuffle along? Or maybe you prefer to sit in the grandstand, cheering on the other runners.

Jesus was a long-distance runner. He was sent to earth by his heavenly Father for a specific task, one that involved a lot of training, sacrifice, and hard work. At the end of his life, as he was hanging on the cross, Jesus said, "It is finished" (John 19:30).

He accomplished what he set out to do. He lived his life to the fullest. He lived it real.

Don't be a lazy Christian, one who is content to amble along through life. Worse yet—don't just watch from the grandstands. Don't be content to listen and congratulate others around you who are running the race with the Lord.

This week put on your tennis shoes and get ready to expel some spiritual sweat. Spend some time loosening up your spiritual muscles and jump into the race set before you.

Why is it easier to live the life of faith from a comfy distance?

What different abilities are needed for a marathon runner versus a sprinter?

How is life more like a marathon than a sprint?

DAY 3

Above all else, guard your heart, for it is the wellspring of life.

Proverbs 4:23

So be careful to do what the LORD your God has commanded you; do not turn aside to the right or to the left. Walk in all the way that the LORD your God has commanded you, so that you may live and prosper and prolong your days in the land that you will possess.

Deuteronomy 5:32–33

Everyone who competes in the games goes into strict training. They do it to get a crown that will not last; but we do it to get a crown that will last forever.

1 Corinthians 9:25

Are you an adrenaline junkie?

If you enjoy things like snowboarding, mountain climbing, bungee jumping, kite surfing, ice diving, mountain bike racing, cliff jumping, or parachuting out of a hot air balloon while juggling and playing the harmonica, then you are a certified adrenaline junkie.

Not to mention the fact that you are one sick individual. And you have my utmost respect. And my prayers. Your parents have my prayers, my respect, and my pity.

What makes a person addicted to extreme sports? What is it that induces an otherwise sane individual to throw caution, as well as their body—strapped to a hang glider—to the wind? Self-proclaimed adrena-

Why Should I Live It Real?

line junkies thrive on adventure, thrills, and the buzz of excitement; their sole ambition is to live life to the fullest. Without any reservation or hesitation.

I want to be an adrenaline junkie. Wait, let me rephrase; I want to be a *Spirit-led* adrenaline junkie. I want to live my life 100 percent for God, trusting in his purpose and plan for my life, without any reservation or hesitation.

One of my favorite bumper stickers is the one that reads,

"Get in, sit down, hold on, and shut up!"

The message is clear: LOOK OUT—HERE WE COME!

OK, so subtract the "shut up" part for a moment. I think it would be a great bumper sticker for those of us wanting to live our lives real for Christ. Without any inhibitions. Without any restraint. Without any worries. With our eyes on God, instead of on ourselves and the problems around us.

It *is* possible to live life to the fullest for God. Let's rephrase our bumper sticker:

"Get in, sit down, hold on, and look up!"

↑ Looking Up

Why does God desire us to live life to the fullest for him?

What kinds of things keep us from living it to the fullest?

What are the benefits of living life to the fullest for God?

DAY 4

You are the light of the world. A city on a hill cannot be hidden. Neither do people light a lamp and put it under a bowl. Instead they put it on its stand, and it gives light to everyone in the house. In the same way, let your light shine before men, that they may see your good deeds and praise your Father in heaven.

Matthew 5:14–16

I, the LORD, have called you in righteousness; I will take hold of your hand. I will keep you and will make you to be a covenant for the people and a light for the Gentiles.

Isaiah 42:6

For you were once darkness, but now you are light in the Lord. Live as children of light.

Ephesians 5:8

Think about what you know about light. Relax, I'm not talking about your latest physics class; let's keep it simple. The main purpose of light is to illuminate or clarify. Some different types of light are lamplight, starlight, firelight, floodlight, candlelight, moonlight, searchlight, spotlight, daylight, stoplight, limelight, sunlight, torchlight, skylight, streetlight, traffic light, flashlight, brake light, strobe light.

Whew, we obviously need light. Why?

To see. To learn. To study. To walk safely. To know truth. And according to the Bible, to see good deeds. Jesus told his disciples to shine their lights before men; Paul admonished the Christians living in Ephesus to live as children of the light.

What's the difference between darkness and light? Ask any four-year-old.

Darkness is scary, unsettling, unknown, cold.

Light is soothing, familiar, warm.

When do most crimes occur? At night, in the dark. When do we have nightmares? At night while we're sleeping. When do most teenagers get in trouble? At night, after curfew.

Satan is the prince of darkness. Jesus is the Light of the World. Light helps us discern the details of something. It helps us recognize flaws. A light can guide or direct us toward safety.

OK, so I've convinced you—light is important. But what does it have to do with living our faith real before others?

Check out the end of Matthew 5:16. It says, "Let your light shine before men, that they may see your good deeds and praise your Father in heaven." As we purpose to live a genuine faith before others, our goal is not to outshine them, or to expose their sin; rather, we are to show them the way, just as you would for a friend lost in the woods in the middle of the night.

And once we've shown them the way to the Father, what will be their response?

Praises to our Father in heaven.

Sometimes the praises are long in coming. My grandmother prayed for my father for fifteen years before he finally saw the Light (sorry, I just can't help myself). But when he finally did, you can be sure he offered praises to his Father in heaven.

You may be a penlight, a floodlight, or a strobe light. Just make sure you are using that light to point others to the true source of light: Son Light.

↑ Looking Up

Have you ever been stuck in the dark without any light? How did it feel?

In what ways does it honor God when you shine his light before others?

Have you ever hidden your light under a bowl?

DAY 5

The apostles said to the Lord, "Increase our faith!"

Luke 17:5

Search me, O God, and know my heart; test me and know my anxious thoughts. See if there is any offensive way in me, and lead me in the way everlasting.

Psalm 139:23–24

Perseverance must finish its work so that you may be mature and complete, not lacking anything.

James 1:4

We sing a lot of great contemporary songs at our church during worship time. I love the rhythm, the beat, the lyrics. But there's nothing like the old hymns. OK, before you write me off as being an old fogey, read the words of my favorite hymn below:

> Be Thou my Vision, O Lord of my heart;
> Naught be all else to me, save that Thou art
> Thou my best Thought, by day or by night,
> Waking or sleeping, Thy presence my light.
>
> Be Thou my Wisdom, and Thou my true Word;
> I ever with Thee and Thou with me, Lord;
> Thou my great Father, I Thy true son;
> Thou in me dwelling, and I with Thee one.
>
> High King of heaven, my victory won,
> May I reach heaven's joys, O bright Heaven's Sun!
> Heart of my own heart, whatever befall,
> Still be my Vision, O Ruler of all.*

Kind of makes you feel holier, with all the "Thou's" and "Thy's," doesn't it? I love this song because it reveals a spiritual maturity that I long to possess someday.

I'll admit that I don't always look to God as my vision. I goof up. I'm not always honest with God, others, or myself. I can be prideful, and choose to serve myself at the expense of others. Too often I walk away from, rather than carry, my cross. I shirk at being discipled. I grieve the Holy Spirit. I ignore God. I choose not to defend my faith. I imitate the world instead of Jesus.

But, oh how I long for God to be my vision! I desperately want to succeed as a believer for him; I don't want to let him down. How

* *Be Thou My Vision*, attributed to Dallan Forgaill, eighth century.

wonderful it would be for God to be our best thought, by day or by night, waking or sleeping, his presence our light.

Since I am in my (ahem) thirties, I've got a little different perspective than you. I know that even though I've matured into full adulthood, my spiritual maturity will take a lifetime. Don't let that fact disappoint you, though. Because, as a Christian, I am continually growing and discovering more about my Lord and Savior.

The reason we should live our faith real is because we are seeking maturity, growth, and spiritual development. Knowing that in our own efforts we will fail miserably, we look to Jesus as our example of how to live the victorious Christian life.

May God bless and keep you as you seek his will and as you live your faith real every day. May your gaze be always drawn toward heaven, with the anticipation of seeing your High King.

↑ Looking Up

What is your favorite worship song?

What actions are you taking to live it real?

How has your life changed as a result of this study?

DAY 6

This is a trustworthy saying. And I want you to stress these things, so that those who have trusted in God may be careful to devote themselves to doing what is good. These things are excellent and profitable for everyone.

Titus 3:8

Therefore, my dear brothers, stand firm. Let nothing move you. Always give yourselves fully to the work of the Lord, because you know that your labor in the Lord is not in vain.

1 Corinthians 15:58

Now to him who is able to do immeasurably more than all we ask or imagine, according to his power that is at work within us, to him be glory in the church and in Christ Jesus throughout all generations, for ever and ever! Amen.

Ephesians 3:20–21

Being real. Being honest.

Tough? Absolutely.

Leslie, everybody's best friend, is the kindest person you've ever seen. She always seems to be happy. She never seems to get stressed. Leslie is loved by everyone who knows her.

You've always wanted to be introduced to Leslie. Not because she's always dressed in the nicest clothes. Not because she seems perfect. But because you're attracted to who she is. Not the outer appearance. Not her popularity. She just radiates something that draws you—and everyone else—to her.

Last week at the track, you finally met Leslie. After you'd finished practicing for the mile relay, you saw Leslie standing by the bleachers waiting for someone. You and a friend walked up to her and said hey. You mentioned that you had some of the same friends. Leslie smiled and said that she'd seen you around, and that she had been wanting to meet you as well.

Since then, you've spent a few hours with Leslie. And even though you were afraid that she wouldn't live up to what you'd observed, your fears turned out to be completely unfounded.

Leslie is amazing. What you observed from a distance has only gotten more real the better you know her. She is selfless, positive, caring, funny, polite, respectful, and fun. She doesn't criticize or talk about people behind their backs; she doesn't brag about herself; she doesn't act superior to everyone else.

The fact is, Leslie is a great person. You can tell that when she says something nice about someone, she really means it. And she doesn't act like a Goody Two-shoes or Miss Priss, like she can't be around certain people.

With everything you've heard about Leslie, you expected that she couldn't be that perfect. Turns out, though, that she really is that good. Leslie lives up to what she appears. Leslie is real.

Do you know anyone like Leslie?

What are the things about Leslie that make her real?

Why is it so difficult to believe that someone as good as Leslie
   exists?

DAY 7

But God chose the foolish things of the world to shame the wise; God chose
the weak things of the world to shame the strong. He chose the lowly things of
this world and the despised things—and the things that are not—to nullify the
things that are, so that no one may boast before him.

1 Corinthians 1:27–29

But thanks be to God, who always leads us in triumphal procession in Christ
and through us spreads everywhere the fragrance of the knowledge of him. For
we are to God the aroma of Christ among those who are being saved and those
who are perishing.

2 Corinthians 2:14–15

But we have this treasure in jars of clay to show that this all-surpassing power
is from God and not from us.

2 Corinthians 4:7

Have you ever counted the cost for following Christ? I bet you have. I
suppose that sometime in your life with Christ you've thought about
how expensive it is to be a Christian. I'm not trying to overdramatize
being a Christian, but think about it (if you haven't already). It costs
something to believe in Christ. Sometimes your friends ignore you,
sometimes your parents harass you, sometimes people openly pick on
you because of your belief.

But think about what you might lose if you weren't a Christian. Better
yet, consider how the people you know would be affected if you didn't

live an honest, open, and devoted relationship with God in front of them. To get a better grasp of how your relationship with God affects those closest to you, do this.

Write on different pieces of paper the names of the following people:

Your three closest friends

Your parents

Your siblings

Now that you have those, lay them out in front of you on the floor. Ask yourself the following questions:

What's at stake in the lives of these people if you aren't real with God?

What would be different in their lives if you weren't fully devoted to God?

What difference does your relationship with God make in their lives?

Do you see the importance of living it real? Do you get how important it is to live a godly life?

Your devotion makes a difference in the lives of the people you love. Your example affects them. Your realness helps them see what a living sacrifice really is. How you live your relationship with God in front of these people makes a difference in them. Through your influence they are more changed, more shaped, and more challenged in their likeness to Christ.

How important is living it real? It's absolutely 100 percent the most important thing you could ever do. So, today think of one way you can model a real relationship to Christ in front of these people. Think of a way you can demonstrate to these people that a real relationship with Christ is the focus of your life and the most important thing they could commit to.

↑ Looking Up

What have you learned about living it real from this activity?

Using what you've learned from this illustration, how would you explain the importance of living it real to your best friend?

How can you apply what you've learned and the truth you've discovered from Scripture about this topic?

Tim Baker is a student ministries leader, an adjunct Bible professor, and the author of numerous student books. Tim lives in Longview, Texas, with his wife and three kids.

Jenn Doucette is a freelance writer, author, and humorist who seeks to encourage others with hope and humor. She is the author of *The Velveteen Mommy: Laughter and Tears from the Toy Box Years* (NavPress, 2005) and *Mama Said There'd Be Days Like This* (Harvest House, 2007). She is currently working on her first novel. Jenn and her husband, Ben, have three children and live in Snohomish, Washington. You can learn more about Jenn by checking out her blog at www.jenndoucette .blog-city.com.